Charles Debrille Poston

Apache Land

Charles Debrille Poston
Apache Land
ISBN/EAN: 9783743351226
Manufactured in Europe, USA, Canada, Australia, Japa
Cover: Foto ©ninafisch / pixelio.de

Manufactured and distributed by brebook publishing software (www.brebook.com)

Charles Debrille Poston

Apache Land

BY

CHARLES D. POSTON,
Of Arizona.

SAN FRANCISCO:
A. L. BANCROFT & COMPANY, PRINTERS.
1878.

Entered according to Act of Congress, in the year 1878,
BY CHARLES D. POSTON,
In the office of the Librarian of Congress, at Washington.

INTRODUCTION.

THERE is not a fictitious name nor a fictitious character in this production. Every incident is founded on fact, which leaves the author but little opportunity for elaboration, even if he had the capacity.

It was written in a mud hut, on a dirt floor; without the advantage of a single book of reference, with no more knowledge of metrical composition than a donkey has of a yard-stick; and goes into the world a simple child of the desert, like the author.

My first personal acquaintance with Apache-Land was in the year 1854, when I made a journey along the eastern coast of the Gulf of California, reaching the Gila river near the Pima villages, and thence by Fort Yuma to San Francisco. Ten years later, in the year 1864, when acting as Superintendent of Indian Affairs for Arizona, an extended tour was made in the southern portion of the Territory, accompanied by my lamented friend, the Honorable J. Ross Browne, who was obliged to leave me at the Pima villages; and I was deprived of the pleasure of his society in the country north of the Gila, and the public of his inimitable sketches and graphic descriptions.

After Mr. Browne's departure I made an expedition to the headwaters of the Rio Verde, accompanied by fifty

Pima and Maricopa Indians, two Opata boys that I had reared, and my Negro cook, Jim Berry (of blessed memory). The Indians were armed with muskets and forty rounds each, which they shot away at coyotes, burro rabbits, crows, and an occasional fleeting deer. It has ever since been a doubt in my mind whether the friendly Indians would not have run away if the Apaches had come down upon us; in which event I should have been left in a very ridiculous position, to say the least of it. In descending the Rio Verde, we passed many cave houses in the rocks on the side of mountains, apparently selected for their inaccessibility, and a little above the confluence of the Verde with the Rio Salado, the ruins of three cities; the central one of which retained the foundations of a very curiously constructed fortification.

The entrance of the Salado at this junction, from this visit and other circumstances, has remained impressed upon my memory as a wild, weird scene, and I have often desired to explore its mysterious cañons. The country north of the Gila, between the Verde and the Rio Grande, is yet comparatively a *terra incognita*, the home of the Apache, and the hope of the miner.

The route over which I passed had been traversed by the Spanish expedition of Coronado three hundred and twenty-two years before, and a graphic description of the country had been given by Casteñada, the historian of the expedition; somewhat more to be relied upon than the fantastic and rather romantic account of Father Mark of Nice, the chaplain; so that although the ground was novel to me, it was nothing new, and is well known to many hunters, trappers, and prospectors, who have unfortunately left no history of their wanderings or of themselves.

After an absence of ten years in foreign countries, the

government of the United States (through the influence of a personal friend) has honored me with the appointment of register of the land office at Florence, at a salary of five hundred dollars a year, as a recompense for my arduous pioneering, and the loss of an ample estate by confiscation and robbery. As there is little or no business in the land office, I could not conscientiously continue to draw the salary punctually every quarter, in installments of one hundred and twenty-five dollars each, without making some effort to show my appreciation of the beneficent intentions of the government.

As the land office at Florence is only allowed one hundred dollars a year for rent, contingent expenses, stationery, fuel, lights, etc., a very small margin remains for obtaining accurate information about a territory containing over a hundred thousand square miles of land. I therefore proposed to the Major-General commanding this Department, to make a reconnoissance of the Salado, from the junction of the Verde to Camp Apache. The general courteously replied that "the proposed investigations, in their bearing upon public interests, are believed to be capable of beneficiary results," and ordered the organization of the expedition as requested, with ample escort and the engineering facilities necessary to determine the value of one of the principal streams of the territory. This reconnoissance will attract considerable attention at St. Louis, and may accelerate our connection with the heart of the United States, where we should look for capital for our mining enterprises, as well as for our commercial supplies.

Having been reared near the banks of Salt river, in Kentucky, and having ascended the classic stream, politically, in Arizona, life would be incomplete without making an effort to explore the stream which has gained so wide a reputation, both among frontiersmen and politicians, and if the expedition results in a benefit to the former, it will be a gratification to have done something for a class of men who are worthy of the highest admiration as the pioneers of civilization; and as for the latter, they will take care of themselves, as they make politics an "industrial pursuit."

CHARLES D. POSTON.

FLORENCE, ARIZONA, 1877.

APACHE-LAND.

APOCHRYPHAL.

On the Sunday before starting, as the expedition was resting in camp, on the left or southern bank of the Salado, a carriage arrived by the Florence road, containing two women; one in the habit of the Sisters of the Sacred Heart at Mt. St. Josephs, near Tucson; the other a Pima Indian, Heh-Wul-Vopuey (the Running Wind).

The Sister (Seraphine) bore traces of more than ordinary beauty, of that peculiar combination of black hair and blue eyes called in Spanish "Morisco." She desired to see the commanding general, and was conducted to his quarters, where the following conversation (principally carried on by the lady) was written down by the stenographer of the expedition:

> Your enterprise we much approve.
> To join it we would dearly love,
> If laws and customs can afford
> Two useful women space on board.
> It may seem like a mystery,
> But wait and hear my history:
> I beg you kindly grant me grace
> In simple measure here to trace
> The strangest life beneath the sun,
> Which brings me here a wandering nun.

I may not claim, without a boast,
Possession of beauty I have lost.
But blood's the genealogical tree
Of nature's true nobility;
And that which courses through my veins,
Came down through not ignoble reins.
My Spanish father—Hidalgo stock—
My mother stole from Tangiers rock.
Hidalgo grafted on the Moor,
You must admit cannot be poor.

Born in Spanish palaces
Guarded by Spanish jalousies,
Watched by my father's sable spoil,
Charged with this care instead of toil,
My childhood passed apace.
In care of kindly Afric race,
Untainted by the world's engaña,
I grew in health in fair España,
Content, as far as life unfurled,
To live in such a pretty world.

But ne'er since Jason sought the Golden Fleece,
Has sailor ever found domestic peace;
Since Ulysses lingered on the love-bound shore,
Have sailors loved the sea far more and more.
Since bold Columbus crossed the Spanish main,
Loved wife and child have ever plead in vain;
And sailors' vows, like sands upon sea-shore,
A moment last and flit forever more.
The tide obliterates lines drawn on sand,
As time wears out vows made upon the land.

Apache-Land.

The orange blossoms of my Spanish home
Were changed for ocean's less enticing foam.
My Moorish mother and our little store
Were next in sight off Afric's sandy shore,
Where Congo freights, and esculent of palm,
Shield traders' traffic in the sons of Ham;
Where oil and ivory offer fair pretense
That human traffic is but innocence;
Where shady palms on Afric's muddy waters
Shield horrid sales of Afric's sons and daughters.

The sable cargo stowed beneath the hatches,
And nice precaution taken with the watches,
In case a British cruiser might be spying
Into the condition of the dead and dying.
Our sails were spread to catch a friendly breeze;
To waft to deeper water—wider seas.
The sun uprose next morning red as blood,
With angry beams pursued us o'er the flood,
Pouring his fiery darts upon the bark
Till his fierce rays were shielded by the dark.

The angry winds lashed ocean's seething foam,
That her fair bosom should be made the home
Of such vile freight, while, poor and harmless, I
Could nothing do except lament and cry.
Oil, ivory, ebony were near eternity,
When love and instinct of maternity,
With inspiration of some mother wit,
Perchance remembrance of some holy writ,
Bids us pour oil upon the troubled waves,
And thus a husband, child and cargo saves.

A month or more, and lovely palms
In Cuban harbor spread their arms
To welcome toilers of the sea,
For sea-worn toilers sure were we;
And by the nurslings of the sun
Ensconced, we fired our signal gun,
When swarthy planters came on board,
Disbursing free their golden hoard,
For men and women whose only crime,
Was birthright in a hotter clime.

The gold doubloons were brought on board,
A sightly and a goodly hoard.
My father took me in his arms,
And pointing out my mother's charms,
Embraced us both, and said that he
Was Spanish Hercules; and she
Was Afric's Queen, and that the twain
Had twined two worlds in love again,
And I the knot that firmly bound,
The pillars from base to top all round.*

Away again from Cuban coasts,
And Spanish laws, and Spanish boasts,
Our prow towards the Spanish main,
Our fleet-winged courser's free again,
And Orinoco's mouth is past,
As down the main she's flying fast,
Till fair Brazil is on the bow,
And Rio's harbor entered now;
Fair city of the Western Sea,
Braganza's Duke is proud of thee.

---

*See the pillars of Hercules on Spanish and Mexican coins.

Away again, our bark struts proud
As peacock showing to a crowd;
Her sails are spread in wanton glee,
For every soul on board is free.
Adown the main, like flying swan,
She rocks, and rolls, and gambols on,
Bowing to every line of coast,
And tossing foam upon the lost,
Till Flores Island comes in view,
Then anchors in Pernambuco.

Refreshed again with ample stores,
We leave the last Atlantic shores;
Our course is bent for Falkland's Isles,
To gather one of fortune's smiles,
Around the Cape of Storms to steer,
With sextant and chronometer.
The stormy cape at last is past,
Of ice and snow we've seen the last;
And now upon Pacific waves,
Her bow and stern our good bark laves.

For Juan's Island, dear to me
From early childish history,
Our prow is set; our sails flow on
Towards the golden setting sun,
Impatient, all in youthful glee,
To wander on the sands, and see
If Friday's track remains in sand,
Or Crusoe still lives on the land;
But Friday's track is washed away,
And Crusoe's dead this many a day.

Tahiti's Islands next are seen,
Rising like mountains capped with green,
And streams are purling through the flowers,
Like music warbling in nature's bowers;
But Christian and his band are gone,
And there remains no living one
To tell us how or when they went,
Or how their span of life was spent;
So these illusions fleet like youth,
And leave us only naked truth.

The Sandwich Islands next were reached,
Where Captain Cook's good ships were beached
And natives feasted wild and high—
Pacific anthropophagi.
From scenes like these we turn away,
And steer our bark for far Cathay,
Where civilization makes her boast
That she was found; but never lost;
For Japan's seas, whose beauty chains
The wildest ranger of the mains.

"Away, away o'er bounding main."
But this is sung, and sung again,
By men the latchet of whose shoe
I am not worthy to undo.
Therefore I'll spare you all the pains
Of following me o'er the mains—
Then Fusi-Yami's towering height
Is the first of Asiatic sight
That greets the toiler of the sea,
Or junketeers from the Yang'tze.

The inland sea of fair Japan
Is fairest scene bestowed on man,
And here forever one might linger;
But for the warning old Time's finger,
Pointing the courses of the sun
That circle eré his race is run:
But for the idol's placid face
That speaks unto the human race:
Prepare ye for eternity,
Time is a fiction—I AM HE!

The palm, the palm, the joyful palm,
God's type of all that's pure and calm.
It stretches forth its shady leaves,
And welcome to the traveler gives.
The nursling of the broiling sun,
It trembles when his course is run,
And under shadow of the night
Hears tales of love, and war, and fight;
Ever compassionate to man,
It shelters him and makes his fan.

On Congo's coast the same flag floats,
It covers many suspicious boats;
And here on fringe of flowery land,
Just where the sea parts from the sand,
Where palm-trees shelter lovely vale,
Floats the great flag of Portugale;
From heights where great Camoens sung,
The banner of his country hung;
In harbor of beautiful Macoa,
Our bark and crew seek shelter now.

Here, Cross and Dragon face to face
With enemies of race to race,
Three hundred years have lived to see
The trade in men, and silk, and tea,
And carnivals of human crime,
Which all the annals of old time,
And records of old revelry,
Could scarcely match in devilry;
And still the flag of Christ floats high,
And flouts against the Chinese sky.

Here, too, in this delicious clime,
Man reckons little of the time;
The gifts of nature freely given
Make him forget all thoughts of heaven;
The orange groves that fringe the land
Drop fruits as golden as the sand,
And flowers as fragrant as can be,
Float perfume o'er the Chinese sea,
An atmosphere so pure and bright
That day is always turned to night.

The sampans dancing on the waters
Are filled with China's olive daughters,
With music of the string and gong,
That rival fabled mermaid's song.
They sing with 'witching minstrelsy:
"Fair, blue-eyed stranger, come with me;
I'll show you China's inland sea,
And almond-eyed girls as fair as she,
Where Canton rivals fair Venice
And nothing can be done amiss."

With music from ten thousand boats
From which the flag of China floats,
The Dragon pointing to the skies
Has diamond tail and mirrored eyes,
Has fins to swim upon the sea,
And legs upon the land has he,
And wings to fly up in the air.
The Lion, crouching in his lair,
Was not so great as China's king,
For he was lord of every thing.

The boats were thick as fish at sea,
And great the wonder was to me,
How they could one another pass;
But each had eyes of looking glass,
For Chinese oarsmen fully know,
"Me no can see, me how can go?"
When in a tempest wild they toss,
They seek to soothe the wrath of "Joss,"
And save themselves from dangers free,
By burning incense on the sea.

The lanterns hang upon the mast,
The sails are set, Whampoa's past,
And close upon the weather lee
A city rises from the sea,
Surpassing all our western towns
In wealth and ornamental grounds.
The pearly river comes to meet
And deck the mistress at its feet,
Washing the banks of fair Shameen,
Pearl island set in emerald green.

Our sampan cast her lines ashore
Before the always open door—
Embowered with China's generous plants
The noble Hong of Olyphants;
For here the strangers always meet
Hosts who with smiles and welcome greet,
On fringe of this great pagan land;
A gentle, kind and Christian band,
Who hospitality bestow
And China's famous city show.

The dishes of a Chinese feast
In cuisine arts outmatch the East.
The watermelon's ripened seed
In general commence the feed;
Then bird's-nest soup in rare tureen
Of richest inlaid porcelain;
Sharks' fins then next apply the test
To stomach of the stranger guest;
A dish of Chinese roasted snails
Requires a glass of stout, or ales.

The ducks are passed by those who live
In China—the cause I cannot give;
But woodcock, fat on Chinese eyes,
Is here an epicurean prize.
Eggs must be stale to grace the feast,
And have a hundred years at least;
For all are taught by Chinese sage,
Respect and duty to old age.
The vinous liquids, always due,
Are rendered in old ripe sam-shu.

The glasses—crystals of the best—
Are fashioned all without a rest;
So guests must at a single quaff
Drain the bottomless goblet off.
The tables groan with all that's nice,
And the feast is closed with curry and rice.
The host then rises from the table,
And if to stand on legs he's able,
Proposes a toast to "absent friends,"
Their absence here to make amends.

The guests then seek the drawing-room,
The fragrant weed in peace to fume,
Till waiters, clad in snowy white,
End entertainment of the night
By serving round small cups of tea,
Distilled from very best bohea—
A beverage not in the number
Of those inclining you to slumber;
And if you'll listen while I try,
I'll try to tell the reason why.

A Buddhist monk oppressed with sin,
Called conclave of the fathers in,
To make confession of his lapse
From virtue—and other things, perhaps.
Before his holy vision strayed
A wanton, frail, fair Chinese maid,
And pinioned in his heart so deep,
A lust that banished balmy sleep,
And raised emotions far from free
Of breaking his celibacy.

The holy fathers pondered well
His wonderful escape from hell,
And made a penance, to be done
From setting to the rise of sun,
That punishment should be inflicted
Upon each member so addicted
To wander from the sphere of duty,
And rest in lust on female beauty;
That through the watches of the night,
His eyes should never close their sight.

The monk upon his penance went;
But ere the morning hours were spent—
Before the hours of night were numbered—
He sat upon his chair and slumbered.
Awaking in astonishment,
He gave his eyes their punishment,
And from his lids their lashes drew;
And on the ground the felons threw,
And stamped them in the earth with feet
In punishment for their deceit.

The hairs consigned to mother Earth
There fructified, and soon gave birth
To stem, soon growing to a tree,
From which the Chinese gather tea.
Thus penances are doing good,
And sermons still are found in wood.
To those who right the riddle read
And would from sleepiness be freed,
Drink strong infusions of the plant—
Your eyes will never slumber want.

The boats are waiting at the door,
The rowers resting on the oar;
The lamps are hung from stem to stern,
The tea is drawing in the urn;
And drapery hung with strange device,
The youth and beauty to entice;
For here in China's inland sea
The nights are given to revelry.
We step aboard; the sampan flies,
And beauty melts from almond eyes.

With music from the sampans flowing
To cadence of the oarsmen rowing,
We float across the pearly waters
In arms of China's lovely daughters;
The lights that glimmer on the sea
Are like the stars of far Chaldee,
And numerous, as. if they meant
To imitate the firmament.
The world's asleep; but we yet live
To suck honey from this human hive.

Our prow is set for fair Shameen
Enshrouded in its dress of green,
Where lanterns, hung on every tree,
Their lights reflected in the sea,
Are rivaled only by the eyes
Of damsels thick as fire-flies,
Who welcome us with mimic fire
Of paper cannon strung on wire,
Draw up their little dainty feet,
And hand a cushion for a seat.

By China's laws and customs old,
The feet of women are controlled.
From infancy to age compressed
In bandage linen, nicely dressed,
They grow no longer than a span.
This was the law of China's Khan,
To settle questions of dispute
Which modern women gravely moot,
In violation of the text
Which sets the status of the sex.

They cannot dance on feet of mice,
And pity 'tis they are so nice,
That boys must play the female part,
In feats of light, fantastic art.
Such are China's laws and rules,
Taught by wise Confucian schools.
But nature has its recompense:
If pressure at the foot commence,
The blood repressed rises high,
And expands itself about the thigh.

We turn us now to fair Shameen,
All glimmering in her garb of sheen,
Whose gardens, lakes and bowers airy,
Invite the gay voluptuary;
The divans rare, of silk brocade,
With China, Tartar, Japan maid,
Invite to bacchanalian feast,
Peculiar customs of the East.
For fear of offending Western law,
We here the silken curtain draw.

The sun rose high o'er Canton towers
Before we left love's shady bowers,
And Shameen's beauties bade farewell,
And Tartar maids who love so well;
Our mandate bids us to Macoa,
Where barque and crew await us now;
The doubloons have been changed for spice,
And some of them for China rice;
Others for sugar and silk and tea,
And varied cargo of the sea:

Sandalwood chairs, bamboo settees,
Fashioned to give the greatest ease,
With furniture around the room,
That spread on board a sweet perfume;
Silk curtains hung about the doors,
And Indian mats upon the floors;
The pantry garnished well again,
With richest, rarest porcelain;
In lieu of Congo ebony,
A load of live mahogany.

We spread our sails and sped along
In sight of peaks of old Hong Kong,
Where British cruisers lie in wait
At gate of China's greatest strait,
Content that we may go and come
If they can smuggle opium ;
Resisting China's wholesome laws,
And making war in holy cause
Of traffic that the devil speeds
In merchandise of poppy seeds.

O God, is there on earth no haven,
No refuge safe this side of heaven,
Where man's inhumanity to man
Is placed beneath the social ban?
Are royal courts, and kings and queens,
In statesmen's hands but puppet means
To guide the people to distress,
To war, and strife, and wickedness?
We'll turn our barque from far Cathay
And seek it in America.

To south south-east we steered our course,
On larboard lee Luchous bold coast,
And passed the Philippean Isles,
Where nature spreads her fairest smiles
To make the land yield plenteously,
To fatten Spanish royalty;
Where poppies and narcotic weed
Rotate the land with changing seed,
Infusing in the mild manilla
An inclination for the pillow.

From here we pointed straight across
A little towards the Southern Cross;
And the first land that we did see,
Bounded the Vermilion Sea;
The promontory of old Saint Luke
Was sighted as if by a fluke.*
The Californian coast extended
As mountains south to south-east trended,
Kind nature's barrier stretched before,
To guard the fair Sonora shore.

---

* Fluke is a sea-phrase.

A landmark here, which all may see,
One foot on land, and one on sea;
Sea-lion, petrified by chance,
Or, monster fixed by Neptune's lance.
It stands where mild Pacific waves
Its legs and body daily laves,
And claims this tribute of the sea
In memory of mastery.
Bold headland, take this small tribute,
Receive, *en passant*, our salute.

Across the sea we fast sailed on,
Abreast the Isle of Tiburon,
Where inlet fashioned in the shore
Sheltered our bark and worldly store.
The sharks abound in Cortez' Sea,
But they shall never feast on me.
Thank God for all the dangers past.
But this long voyage is our last;
For anchored on Sonora's shore,
We leave the sea for evermore.

The island where our good ship lies,
Is isle of sharks—as its name implies;
Inhabited by a dusky race
A trifle yellow in the face,
And gifted with a nature savage,
The adjacent coasts and towns to ravage,
But where, or whence they came, indeed
Would puzzle students much to read.
Their origin's a mystery
To chronicles or history.

Most venomous reptiles here abound
And make the isle forbidden ground,
To all except this savage race
Who keep up here their hiding-place.
They place these reptiles in a pit,
And lash them till they madly spit
Their venom in a tiburon's liver,
Which, placed in bottom of a quiver,
Infuses in the arrow's point,
And sinews that confine the joint,
A poison rank, and, shot by stealth,
The Ceris' arrow's certain death.

They're like the Asiatic race
In indications of the face;
In speech, our Chinese servants could
With trouble slight be understood.
This isle has formed them safe refuge,
Perhaps, e'er since the great deluge.
With boat and spear they gather fish,
And cook them in an earthen dish
With salt, and other things in store
Gathered from the adjacent shore.

The cargo landed on the strand,
My father bought a caravan,
And silk and tea and miners' tools
Were laden on the stout pack-mules.
The ship, dismantled, rides upon
The sea; a grinning skeleton;
Stripped to the ribs, it floats alone;
It floats a ghost the sea upon,
One kiss I waft unto the sea,
For thousands she has given me.

With foot firm placed upon the land,
I join the moving caravan,
To seek in Arizona mountains
The fabled sources of youth's fountains;
Ascending higher unto God,
Where never foot of man has trod;
A home more stable than the sea,
With those who are the world to me.
And there amongst the scenes primeval,
I surely never can see evil.

Rivers run to the sea, their sources the sky;
Wide enough at the mouth, but narrow on high.
And all those who strive to make the ascent,
Must often remember the New Testament
In parables teaching, which difficult seem;
One goes easier down than up any stream.
But all we can do is to do our *devoir*,
For not all the climbers can cry "Excelsior."
Our duty is done, if we fall by the way;
Look upward forever; praise God and pray.

The caravan moved on apace,
And even those of brutish race
Gathered inspiration by the way,
And vented it in cheerful neigh;
The mules pricked up their ears, and kept,
With jingling spurs, a steady step.
The cruppers fastened close behind,
The hackamore upon the blind;
The broad belt-cinch and shoulder-brace
Kept aperajo in its place.

In camp at night the watch-fires burned;
The mules and horses loose were turned
In low foothills and mountain pass,
To graze upon the grama grass.
The camp-fire burned a ruddy hue,
The sky above was gold and blue.
All nature seemed to take delight
In the still watches of the night.
Our Tartar tent was pitched on high,
To shed effulgence of the sky.

The venison steaks were cut and broiled,
Our Chinese servants sweat and toiled
The guajolote rich to roast
And baste his breast with buttered toast;
To stuff him with the rich castaña,
Which grows here in this New España;
The mountain quail which here we found,
Were roasted on a willow wand,
Which gives the bird an unctuous flavor,
And very palatable savor.

The bear's oil forms a dressing nice,
When flavored with some eastern spice,
And spread upon the turkey's wing,
Makes dish to set before a king;
A bullock's head was cut and dressed,
The blood from out its vessels pressed;
A hole was fashioned in the ground
And firmly set with stones around,
The heat and juice to smother in,
And then the head was put within.

A large flat stone was placed on top,
And fire was kindled on the rock,
To roast the head within the skin
And keep its juicy flavor in,
So that by streak of early morn
It might be lifted by the horn
And made a matutinal meal
With relish citizens never feel.
The sentinels their vigils kept,
Whilst we in camp securely slept.

The camp at morn was early stirred
That we might match the early bird,
For who like sluggards slept too late
Would miss their morning chocolate.
The packs were spread upon the ground
In systematic circle round;
The mules, with instinct of the brute,
Each found his own day-harness suit
And stood aside, upon his back
To receive his daily 'customed pack.

The blind is first placed o'er his eyes
To shield them from the biting flies;
A sudoriento next the skin,
To take the perspiration in;
A matting made of soft maguey;
Then aparejo stuffed with hay,
Its ends expanding very wide,
To guard the patient pack-mule's side;
The pack is then securely cinched
Until the mule has groaned and winced.

The load is then placed on the pack,
Adjusted fairly to the back,
And safely round the belly tied
With ropes and thongs of stout rawhide,
The muleteer, or p'raps the dueño,
Slaps mule on hip, and cries out "Bueno."
The mule steps quickly to the road,
Soon as he fairly gets his load,
Which should in reasonable bounds
Not much exceed three hundred pounds.

A gray mare leads the cavallada,
Is mistress of the whole mulada;
For here, as in other lands, of course,
"The gray mare is the better horse."
With jingling bell which music made,
She leads the lively cavalcade;
Her bell, and hide so very white,
Form safeguard either day or night;
For mules, like sheep on highland heather,
Are always led by a bell-wether.

The riders strike with spur and whip
A lagging mule upon the hip;
And oft in rugged mountain road,
Have trouble to adjust the load.
My father rode an Arab steed—
Or, at the least, a full half breed—
Whose foam was white as mountain snow
On atlas peaks in Morocco;
The saddle, formed by Spanish art,
Was perfect in its every part.

The pommel, projecting at the front,
Was garnished with a silver mount,
The stirrup fashioned like a boat,
Made large and wide, to ease the foot,
And these were shining bright, brand new;
And they were silver-mounted too;
The bit was from my mother's land,
So fashioned that a single strand
Of silk could guide the wildest steed
That ever came of Moorish breed.

With jingling spurs that music kept,
And helped the mules to keep the step,
My mother and I, in silk sedan,
Kept pace with the moving caravan;
Four coolies trotted by our side,
To take the chair when others tired,
Until the shadow of the sun
Reminded us 'twas time to noon;
When, stopping by a mountain side,
We camped in valley green and wide.

Beneath a grove of cottonwoods,
We made our camp and stacked our goods,
For where this kind of timber grows,
You may be sure the water flows.
In camping, 'tis considered meet
To have a valley at your feet,
With abundant grass for stock to eat,
And a mountain back for safe retreat;
Let watch be placed upon a rise,
To guard the camp against surprise.

In fashion thus we journeyed on,
From rising till the set of sun,
Till at the end of some two weeks
We came in sight of mountain peaks
Which, pointing to the sky with snow,
Gave warning to no further go;
And finding here a valley wide,
Guarded by mountains on each side,
We pitched our tent beside a lake
Which rivers from the mountains make.

The Indians call it Arivac;
About ten leagues from old Tubac,
Where Spaniards, hundred years ago,
Established a Presidio,
And twenty leagues from old Tucson,
Where Jason took his gold fleece from;
For in the annals of old time,
Which sadly puzzle modern rhyme,
It's spelt "Toison," which means a piece,
The Spanish knights of golden fleece.

At any rate, we settled here;
And scared away the timid deer,
And scared away the civet cat,
To make this place our Ararat.
My father built an altar stone,
And sacrificed a goat thereon,
In burning incense to the sun,
That such a happy home we'd won;
The smoke ascended straight to heaven,
As Indian's strongest shot had riven.

ARIVACA

Here home was found—a very home;
No more on treacherous seas we'll roam;
But here, on virgin soil of God,
We'll live by turning up the sod,
And cultivate the land for bread,
As all who Holy Writ have read,
Must know the sons of Adam's doom
From erst, the cradle to the tomb.
Here sheltered from the world, we three,
Wife, husband, child—EARTH'S TRINITY.

With stone, and lime, and lofty pine,
And much material from the mine,
Foundations laid by square and rule,
And lofty cellars deep and cool,
A "casa" rose above the plain—
Its like we'll never see again.
The bricks were burnt out in the sun,
Just as of old in Babylon;
And straw was furnished to concrete
The mass in shape both square and neat.

The lofty pines were cut and squared,
And in the burning sun well aired,
To underlie the house's floors;
Mesquite was polished for the doors;
And windows, made in convex form
To guard the casa from the storm,
Were interlaced with iron bars
For ventilation—and for wars.
In front, a great long colonnade
The soft red yielding porphyry made.

The quarries found on the estate
Yielded a hard and dark blue slate,
Which made a handsome Mansard roof,
Both water-tight and fire-proof.
At angle facing eastern sun,
We raised a lofty torreon,
And mounted there our cannons high,
In relief against the eastern sky;
From nomads north put on our guard—
We must ever here keep watch and ward.

Our house outside was rough to view,
And finished with rude stucco;
But inside, furnished from the floor
To attic with the richest store
Of furniture that Europe boasts,
Or yield the fair Atlantic coasts
With garniture of Asian skill
And quaint device of Hindoo will;
Fine Cashmere shawls adorn the walls
And Japan's bronzes fill the halls.

Persian rugs are on the floors,
And Chinese silks enshroud the doors—
The windows hung with tapestry,
Of Gobelin's famous factory;
And porcelain, the finest make
Of China's famous Poyong lake.
The Aztec's clumsy golden plate
Was set beside the Sévres state.
Native silver formed the staff,
And ornamented the carafe.

Our wines were wines of Portugal,
And native drink of old Mescal,
With goodly store of French champagne
Which we had brought o'er many a main,
And Burgundy which since the flood
Has enriched the sons of Noah's blood;
Chablis, for use upon the sea ;
Cognac, to temper with the tea—
In Russian fashion it is made
And commonly called a " citronade."

Our store of sherry is, of course,
Abundant. For my father's use,
Absinthe is served when we guests invite,
To titillate the appetite ;
And after dinner Roman punch
(The stout and ales are served at lunch);
The coffee, which I most admire,
Is roasted on a mesquite fire,
And stirred about with willow sticks,
Half Mocha, and half Java, mixed,

Then ground to color of the opal,
The best mills come from Constantinople.
About the pot there's great dispute,
But Veyron's patent seems to suit;
Distilling essence drop by drop,
And leaving grounds up in the top.
Sugar and cognac stirred about;
If you like, you burn the spirit out.
After this, in regulated homes,
The ladies retire to drawing-rooms.

Our beds were stuffed with feathers plucked
In Norway, from the eider duck,
And placed on steads from far Cathay,
Made of the best mahogany,
With silken curtains hung about
To shut the glaring sunlight out.
The tester, hung with Indian punkas,
Was pulled by oriental flunkies,
Who through the night their cadence kept,
And fanned us while we sweetly slept.

The docile natives came around
To help us plant and till the ground,
In accord with laws that nature made,
That all who live should work for bread,
Each in his proper sphere, of course;
For mule can't do the work of horse,
Any more than man who has to labor
Can get along without his neighbor;
On land as well as on a ship
There's a kind of forced co-partnership.

The Indians here are called Pimos—
In writing, it is spelled Pimas;
For Jesuit fathers undertook
Of Pima tongue to make a book,
And composed a Pima dictionary
For acolytes about to carry,
The text of which, sent back to Spain,
Is preserved in convent San Augustine;
From a copy which my father brought,
The Pima language soon was taught.

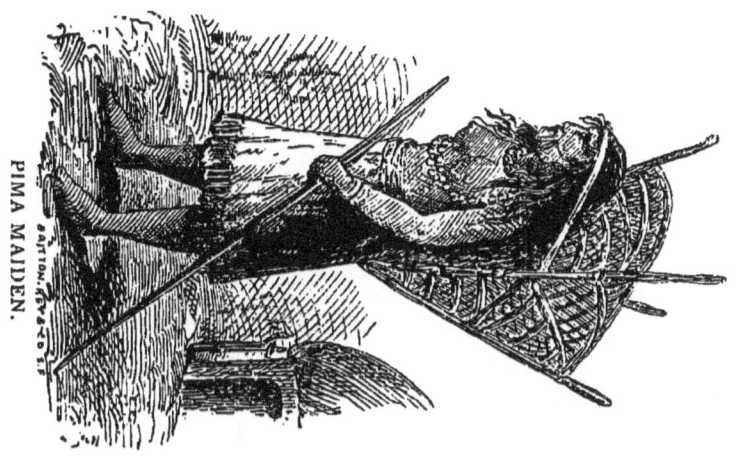

PIMA MAIDEN.

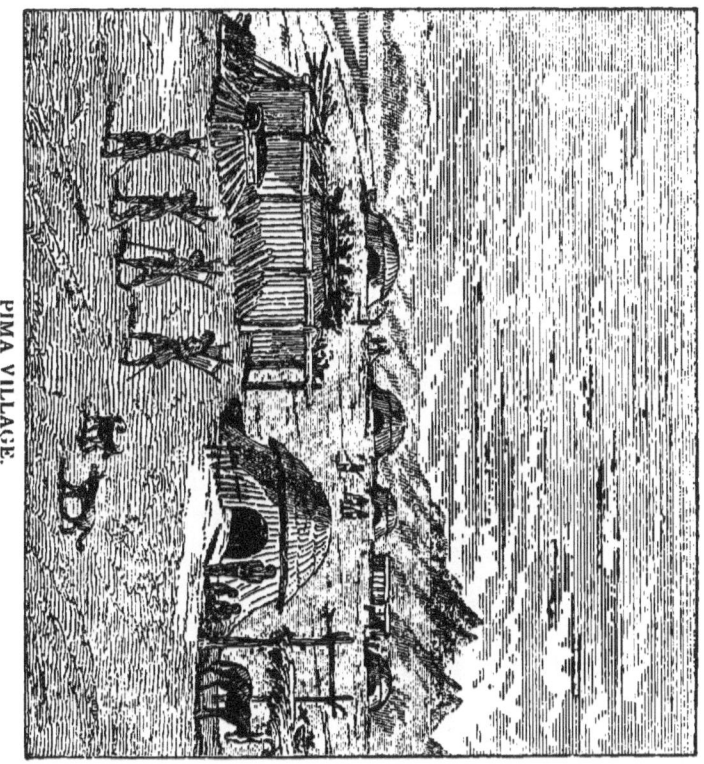

PIMA VILLAGE.

The men were placed to herd on lea,
The girls left to my mother and me;
They learned to cook and make the tea,
With simple kinds of broidery;
They appeared as simple as a child,
Daughters of Eve without a guile.
They poked their noses 'gainst the glass,
And laughed because they would not pass;
Surprised, in simple, childlike glee,
They couldn't touch what they could see.

The Pima race inhabits most
Of the country north of Sonora coast;
From Gila's northern boundary
To eastern shore of Cortez' sea.
Their houses once were grand and high;
And yet, in Arizona's sky,
When passing on the Tucson road,
The ruins of a king's abode
Are seen upon the eastern plain;
Or perhaps it was a pagan fane.

The Pima's name's much controverted,
And many remain still unconverted
To this or that man's theory,
As we learn naught of history.
You ask a Pima how to go,
Or something that he does not know,
He's sure to answer you "pima'-ch;"
If favor's asked, he says "pia'-ch,"
For Pimas are a stingy race,
And have a kind of Jewish face.

A part of the great Pima tribe
Have parted from the mother hive,
And try, in some half-Christian way,
Their duties to the church to pay;
They may be known by wearing clothes,
And somewhat less of Hebrew nose;
They worship at old San Xavier,
But their piety is not severe.
The rest, who flout the church's livery,
Live westward from Mount Babaquivera.

They here tend flocks of cattle and sheep
Until Sonora farmers reap
Their rich, abundant trigo's yield,
When they're employed in harvest field;
In Winter they come to Arivac,
The woman always with the pack
Of household goods in rawhide sack,
With small papoose upon her back,
Convenient to the founts of lac,
Which modest covering always lack.

The men engage in hunting game.
The antelope, not very tame,
Is caught by many crafty tricks,
Which only Indian skill can fix;
They take the half a skin of one,
And carefully dry it in the sun,
The hide all stiff, the horns erect;
The vacant eyes, their eyes protect,
When creeping slyly through the bush,
Or in the heat of chase they rush.

Then clothe themselves with shirt blood-red,
And fix the skin about their head;
Then sally out to catch the game,
Which roams with such romantic name.
The herd, astonished at such sight,
Confounded, lose their senses quite;
An antelope with shirt blood-red,
And skin and horns about his head,
Is vision to excite surprise,
And fascinates their pensive eyes.

They stand like statues on the plain,
Whilst wily hunter takes his aim,
When "bang" goes rifle, and a buck·
Falls to the ground, in vitals struck;
The herd, all heedless of the gun,
All gather round the stricken one;
Not like some deer, and people too,
Who run away when dangers brew;
The hunter loads his gun again,
And piles the plain up with the slain.

The women do domestic work;
Their lords and masters ape the Turk,
And have but slight felicity
In matters that domestic be.
They gather willows from the lake,
And pretty willow baskets make,
Painting the outside clean and nice,
With varied, strange, and quaint device;
Cementing some with gum mesquite,
To keep the water pure and sweet.

They gather clay from out the ground,
And in a mortar finely pound,
Then mix with water from the lake,
Until the mass will fashion take;
Then twirling it around their hands
In many circumfluent bands,
They fashion it in form desired,
To make utensils as required;
Then place it in the sun to dry,
And paint it with the charcoal's dye.

The crocks are taken from the sun,
And great, long furnace placed upon,
The jars and pans and oven's lid
Forming a little pyramid.
The fuel to heat this crucible
Was ordure from the horse corral;
For stronger heat the pots would crack,
And charcoal likely burn them black.
Thus Nature teaches for her part
These simple-minded people art.

The Mission Church of San Xavier
Deserves a little notice here.
A pretty ground it stands upon,
Three Spanish leagues from old Tucson;
The waters of the Santa Cruz
Lend here the church their willing use,
Then sink themselves upon the plain,
And ne'er are used by man again.
Its walls were built, as records show,
About two hundred years ago.

The Jesuits, for the love of Christ,
Their lives and pleasures sacrificed,
And here, as elsewhere, monument
Excites your greatest wonderment,
That this wild wilderness of sin
So grand a structure should be in.
Its domes and towers rising high,
Its cross uplifting to the sky;
But here, indeed, it grandly rose,
The Mecca of the Papagos.

This name was given them by priests
In testimony of release
From Lucifer, and all the hells
Where soul of unshrived Pima dwells.
The fathers well knew how to build.
With unmatched architectural skill
They searched the country with the aid
That travel and experience made,
And with their scientific lights
Selected the best building sites.

They laid it off by square and rule,
And sunk a crypt both deep and cool,
For revery and safe deposit,
A treasury and study-closet:
The foundations were well laid with stone
Brought from the mountains one by one,
In ox-carts fashioned stout and good,
With beds of hide and wheels of wood.
Cement was made of water and lime,
A concrete mass defying time.

Of sun-burnt brick were made the walls,
Plastered with lime the inner halls;
The parapet, and towers thick,
Were finished off with kiln-burnt brick;
The dome surmounted all—on high,
A very model of the sky.
My mother loved the Moorish towers,
In memory of happier hours,
And pronounced the *tout ensemble* scenic,
The architecture Saracenic.

The walls, adorned with holy frescos,
The altars, picturesque reredos,
Were work of some Italian priest,
Who studied art in the far East;
The candelabra on the altar,
And urn, to hold the holy water,
Were made of solid pina plata;
Abundant here midst other matter.
In San Xavier I love to linger
And muse on march of old Time's finger;

For here, with Christ in holy union,
It was I took my first communion.
Full many sorrows since I've seen,
In many dangerous places been;
But vision of Christ upon the sea
Has comfort always brought to me;
For faith, and hope, and charity,
Will win the gate of heaven—these three.
Then Christ will see the little child,
And forgive all after errors wild.

The work has sped at Arivac .
With plow and spade, and hoe and ax;
The ground's been turned and seed insown,
Of barley, wheat, and Indian corn;
With beans, and peas, and black frijol,
And seed of lovely marigold;
The garden's sown with native legumbres,
And foreign plants in endless numbers,
With melon seeds from Spain and Cuba,
And natives from the banks of Yuba.

The orchard's set with tropic fruits,
With peach, and pear, and apple shoots;
Sonora figs, and Altár dates,
And trees, imported from the States;
With seed of always rich banana,
Brought from plantations at Havana;
Citron and orange of every clime,
Not even forgot the useful lime;
For orange, I eat the mandarin,
Because 'tis easy stripped of skin.

The vineyard, on south mountain-side,
Was plowed in rows 'bout two feet wide;
Planted with vine-slips from Sonora,
Del Moreno, "El Aurora,"
And from Los Angeles and Sonoma—
California grapes all lack aroma.
We had China vine-slips in the bark,
By sons of Shem saved from the ark.
'Tis said that wine inspires the muse,
But to rhyme these vines—it is no use.

To fructify this planted crop
And make the seeds with vigor hop,
The great necessity is water,
Which is said, by those who "hadn't oughter,"
To be as scarce as good society—
A slander, lacking in variety.
To irrigate the fields and plains,
In country where it never rains
And water *is* a scarcity,
Is work of prime necessity.

We dammed the streams on mountain-sides,
And made canals for water-guides,
Trained through the fields to gently flow;
And when they needed overflow,
Opened the dikes and water-gates,
And through the ground it percolates
In vivifying streams, and gains
A better crop than meager rains;
For ancients taught us long ago,
This was the way to make crops grow.

Mother and I must have our space,
And claimed a little garden-place
Just by the house, quite close at hand,
To plant with shrubs from Flowery Land,
And seeds of every kind of flowers,
With vines for aromatic bowers;
We inclosed it with a cactus hedge,
Which grew as thick as they could wedge,
Making a fence impervious
To animals, and to the dust.

Inside, the cactus hedge to screen,
A bois d'arc hedge fringed it with green;
And inside this, to further please,
A row of Chinese orange trees,
From which a bounteous nature showers
Delicious fruit and fragrant flowers;
The China asters next were seen,
Dwarf firs in pots for evergreen;
Japonicas set out in rows,
The ever-lovely English rose.

Upon the center of the ground
The Chinese gardeners raised a mound
With taste unique and cunning skill,
The smaller flowers in plats to fill.
Surmounting all, a noble fount
Shed jets of water from the mount.
In this mundane elysium
We found relief from tedium,
And innocently passed the hours
In needlework, 'midst fruits and flowers.

The summer past, the autumn come
Which brings us to our harvest-home,
When reapers gathered bounteous measure
Of golden fruits of earthly treasure,
The Papagos, to share the yield,
The gleaners followed in the field.
The granary was filled with wheat,
Which in the soil grows rich and sweet;
The corn was stacked up in the field—
The store-rooms would not hold the yield.

In gratitude for this abundance
And nature's bounteous redundance,
My father, after his siesta,
Made plans with us for a fiesta,
Which we should give his farm colleagues
Who lived within a hundred leagues.
They had to us been very kind,
And sent us every breed of kine,
With fowls of every quality
In rural hospitality.

Mother and I inscribed the list
Of guests invited to the feast.
To give full time to viands seek,
The feast was set for Christmas week.
Our nearest neighbor on the north
Douglass, who at Sopori held forth—
A man of old Virginia's school,
Who here o'er Mexicans held rule.
The next place north of old Tubac
Was Mission San Xavier del Bac,

Whose curé must of course have place
At head of board, to ask the grace.
Tucson's convives appreciate
A dinner served on silver plate:
But north of this a thousand miles
Are only savage Indian wilds.
We turn us south up Santa Cruz
And find Americans who use
The social laws—and nothing lack,
At presidio of old Tubac.

RUINS OF THE MISSION OF TUMACACORI

Thence passing Mission Tumucacori
One league, about the break of day,
Next Calabazas comes in view,
A fine old Jesuit ruin too:
Then turning south, 'cross the divide
Where savage Indians lurk and hide,
To intercept—perhaps to slaughter—
The traveler at Zarca's water,
We meet at Imuriz an Alemann,
The blue-eyed Saxon, Hulsemann.

At Magdalena, fast or feast,
The traveler's a welcome guest;
Gonzales' board is always spread
With best of meat and wine and bread,
Served by his mozos all sedate,
Upon a set of silver plate.
His beds are built of shining brass,
And covered with a hair mattress.
My father knew him long ago,
Where Congo River's waters flow.

The hacienda "la Alamitta,"
A name and place both very pretty,
Owned by old Mañuel Yñego,
Who's dead and gone long ago,
Was named for an invited guest;
And here we'll stop at night and rest.
The old fox lived a scandalous life,
Unmatched except by his own wife.
The sons, 'tis said, are dreadful rakes,
But invited for their sisters' sakes.

At "La Labor," the next in train,
We found the noble Aztissirain,
A gentleman in every part—
In mind and soul and mien and heart;
In travels quite a wanderer.
Now son-in-law of Guadara,
He cultivates estates paternal,
And with solicitude maternal,
Accepts the willing patronage
Of a thousand held in peonage.

At Tapahua, next upon the round,
The governor of the State is found,
Don Manuel Maria Guadara;
Whom not the vilest slanderer
Is found to say a word against,
Or bring the slightest charge fornenst.
He lives in patriarchal state,
His faithful Yaquis guard his gate;
The stranger's welcome to his hall,
He's "the noblest Roman of them all."

We next must visit l'Hermosilla
To wait on Dona Maria Emparra,
The chief senora of the place,
Whose most unfortunate disgrace,
A naughty husband, lives afar;
So she's consoled by Aguilar.
Her niece, fair Senorita Goerlitz,
Child of a Russian scamp from Oerlitz,
Another family disgrace,
Which happened down about San Blas.

Guaymas, a dirty little port;
Aduana Cuartel, an old mud fort,
The home of land and water rats
Living in homes unfit for bats,
Engaged in commerce contraband,
Disgrace to either sea or land.
Haciendero's feasts are never made
For persons only known in trade.
In Guaymas town, the only man
To invite, "el Consul American."

The Ainsa family are invited,
For else we fear they'll think they're slighted;
A family of Manilla race
With type of Asiatic face.
The girls are rather interesting,
The boys you're never done detesting,
Because they have such peacock ways
And always speak in their own praise;
But Augustine we think must go,
To please his caro, Amelia Yñigo.

The list is finished down so far,
We now return to high Altar,
Where Zepada rules the social roast
And busies him about the coast;
And neighbors say he's quite gone mad
About the port of Libertad.
A Ciudadano true is he,
And first in every charity;
His wife and daughter quite *au fait*
In graceful hospitality.

Our nearest neighbor's Jose Moreno,
The young and very handsome dueño
Of the best hacienda in Sonora,
And very rightly named Aurora;
Where agriculture's well conducted,
And peon labor is instructed
In use of patent implements
Instead of native simplements.
His horses roam in countless drove,
A thousand hills his cattle rove.

This is, from Guaymas to Tucson,
All who are classed as *gente de raison*.
Another question rises yet,
Involving frontier etiquette:
The Indian chiefs in neighborhood
Have often sat at father's board;
Omitted now, they might take slight;
And think they were not treated right.
Old Anton Azul, the Pima chief,
Is a good old man, but very deaf.

A Papago's name would load a horse—
Jose Antonio Victoriano Solorse,
He holds his court at San Xavier,
And when we've passed gave us good cheer.
Those Spanish dons are proud of place,
Punctilious about their race;
The ladies, too, might feel unpleasant
If these untutored Los were present.
So, for fear of running 'gainst good taste,
We'll not decide this case in haste.

THE SAGUARA

We spared no pains in preparation,
To render this, our first oblation,
Full worthy of our rank and station,
And give our neighbors delectation.
The fruit of many cacti serves
To make most excellent preserves,
Mixed with indigenous miel,
Which Papagos in bottles sell,
Made of the fruit of the seguarro,
A name which Indians only borrow.

The rightful name is the "petiyah,"
For trees that grow a little higher;
Or, if you learned books discuss,
'Tis "Cereus giganteus"—
A tree which grows in desert lands,
And finds its nurture in the sands;
It rises limbless fifty feet,
Yielding a fruit both rich and sweet;
And when the fruits quite ripened fall,
The Papagos hold carnival.

They gather it for winter's use,
And from the pulp express the juice,
Obtaining, as I try to tell,
A very palatable miel.
The pulp is then compressed in cakes,
And very dainty bread it makes.
The oak here yields its rich bellotas,
And in the ground are found camotas—
The germ of our own sweet potato,
Though cultivation improves its nature.

The ammabroma sonorea
Grows freely in the Papagueria,
But can scarce be called an esculent—
A kind of waif, by nature sent,
To feed the dwellers in the sand,
On western shores of Sonoraland.
A bread is made from the acacia,
An astringent kind of food called "pach'tea,"
With piñons, tunas, and nogale;
Of fruits, sylvester forms finale.

Our preparations all were made,
And stores exhaustless were inlaid,
To close the year with song and dance
And gratitude for our advance
In prosperity and social state,
And all the joys that should elate
The prosperous to give a feast
At end of every year, at least;
We spread our gates, adorned our walls,
And decked with evergreens our halls.

The alameda long and wide,
With cottonwoods to shade each side,
Stretched out a good long mile, or more,
An avenue to the front door.
O'er water trained in streams to meet
Beneath stone bridge at end of street,
"Bien venido" welcomed guest
To hospitality and to rest.
The cannon thundered from the towers
A welcome to these guests of ours.

Old Douglass came like old King Cole,
As guests arrived in days of old,
With fiddlers and with harpers three,
To add to our festivity.
The curé of San Xavier del Bac
Came mounted on a palfrey's back,
With Tucson's gallants in his train;
And Commandanté Commoduran,
The Tubac chief, came, with his band,
In an ambulance with four-in-hand.

There are some meetings like a doom,
That follow us unto the tomb.
To mother in the colonnade,
This Tubac chief obeisance made,
And kissed my hand in greeting meet;
I trembled then from head to feet.
But what of this? Our guests require
The welcome courtesy of my sire,
His wife's kind greetings all the while,
And not the least his daughter's smile.

The Tubac chief brought in his band
The natives of most every land;
But not for him these sketches made;
For what is he, to Sonora maid?
Bat for their own intrinsic worth,
I must in duty set them forth:
First, Ehrenberg, a Saxon mild,
Who had in youth been very wild,
And ranged in Texas border wars
Until his face was full of scars.

Thence wandering far to Oregon,
He earned his way with trap and gun;
From thence he sailed to Sandwich Isles,
Where he was employed by Minister Wiles
To make survey of Honolulu,
And paint eruption of Tululu,
Whence he sailed to island Otaheite,
Where, 'tis said, he was Queen Pomaré's deity;
How this may be we must not scan—
He was an interesting man.

Brunckow, of name and type quite Russian—
His mother was a native Prussian—
In German scientific lore,
He learned to analyze the ore,
And with a mere blow-pipe assay,
Find out how much a mine would pay;
He came from Texas over here,
To search for mines or chase the deer;
In manners he a Frenchman quite,
Extremely well-bred and polite.

Schuchard was a native Hessian,
A draughtsman able by profession;
And led by fortune out this way,
On the first Pacific Railroad survey;
His steady gaze I could not endure,
For fear he'd make my caricature.
A fellow of most wondrous wit,
Who oft with pencil made a hit
Which pen or words cannot describe,
But they ne'er forget who feel the gibe.

Methner, Besler, and other Dutchmen—
You have no interest in such men,
They just know how to smoke the pipe;
But Kuestel was of Magyar type,
And learned in best Hungarian schools
To use assay and mining tools.
His sister, and niece, the fraulein Kline,
Were company for those at the mine.
The fraulein, a most accomplished person,
Inspired, somehow, a great aversion.

Pumpelly, prince of mining men,
Completes the list of Tubac's ten,
Who came to join our festive board,
And render praise to harvest Lord.
If one's omitted where you've read,
'Tis in sacred memory of the dead;
The Pima Indians teach you this,
And always take it quite amiss
To question them about a brother
Who's gone where angels round him hover.

Hulsemann came with old Torafio,
The Gonzales name is all engafio;
My father knew him on Congo's coast,
And here they meet as guest and host,
To talk of ventures of the sea,
And ante-nuptial revelry.
They drove a pair of spanking bays,
And others led for fresh relays;
Torafio traveled in great state,
And carried with him silver plate.

The Yñigos came with grand escort
Of Indian lancers, like cohort
Of ancient soldiers, trained to wield,
On horse or foot, the spear and shield;
The Aztissirains, with ample train,
In carriage that was brought from Spain;
The governor's guard, a hundred Yaquis—
As soldiers you'll not find their matches;
They've stood by him in all his wars,
And carry many ugly scars.

The fat old Doña Maria Emparra,
With pretty niece, came in a carro,
Bringing along, with part her train,
A handsome young American;
The Ainsas came in shabby plight,
Reminding us of adage trite—
In pride and poverty partnership,
There's sometimes good companionship;
The Morenos and Zapedas together
Arrived like other birds of feather.

After the usual salutations,
Our guests were taken to different stations,
Their attendants placed in proper quarters,
And horses led to drink the waters.
They all arrived by Noche-bueno,
The Christmas eve of Americano,
In time to change their dusty costumes,
And join with us in Christian customs,
While Father Escalante read,
And the church's blessing on us spread.

On Christmas morn, at rise of sun,
The hour was told by peal of gun,
Which, sounding from the mountain peaks,
Waked echoes in the valley creeks,
Announcing here, in place forlorn,
The day the Son of God was born.
The greetings made, a mass was said,
And then the festive board was spread;
My part was first to brew a grog
Americans mix and call egg-nog,

The chief components milk and brandy;
But if you've not the cognac handy,
Good whisky serves as substitute,
Or rum, or juice of maguey root.
The milk must first be thoroughly sweetened,
Then yolk of eggs as thoroughly beaten;
The whites are whipped to make the foam,
Some nutmeg to adorn the comb;
Then serve in goblets, and the rest
Is "Merry Christmas" to your guest.

Arrangements had been made before,
To have the fish brought from sea-shore,
And oysters, which are now in season,
With turtles, to make soup to feast on;
The rancho furnished beef and mutton,
With pigs enough for any glutton;
And hunters had been hired, to grace
Our board with trophies of the chase—
With deer, and antelope, and bear,
And turkeys wild—the best of fare.

The way to roast an ox for feast,
Is whole to barbecue the beast;
And turkeys should be cooked entire,
In a very hot but smothered fire;
The intestines lend the bird a flavor,
The burning feathers give it savor.
The blood of every meat for use,
Forms nature's best, most natural juice;
Of French *ragout* and English roast,
We do not care at all to boast.

Our Christmas dinner passed off well,
With incidents we need not tell;
Each guest was seated by a mate,
To add to pleasures of the plate,
The spice congenial company gives,
When formal dinner it relieves,
Enhancing greatly talk and zest,
Which gen'rous host desires for guest;
For else a dinner's wholly spoiled,
The pleasures of the day assoiled.

The wines were served from crystal stoup,
A little sherry after soup;
Chablis with fish, next after which
The drink was claret, red and rich;
Champagne, of course, was served with game.
All dinners are about the same,
And after a while the men got prosy,
When the ladies retired to have a cozy;
For while they linger o'er the port,
We, too, must have our little sport.

For outdoor sports throughout the days,
We improvised some little plays.
A chicken cock placed in the ground
At outer edge of the race-course round,
His head projecting from the mound,
Formed mark for horsemen sweeping round,
Who stooped from saddle-bow to ground,
And oft a tumbled rider found
His equestrian ability
Outmatched by cock's agility.

The Yaquis gave their native dance
In circle gathered round the lance,
At center firmly set in ground,
With pennons spread the circle round,
Their anklet, shells of rattlesnakes,
In dancing a wild cadence makes;
While song, invented for the hour,
In fashion of the troubadour,
In verse lampooned each noted guest,
With hits that brought the laugh and jest.

All day, serapé spread on ground,
The gambling groups may here be found
Indulging in a monte game
Of cards, of ancient Aztec fame.
Inveterate gamblers are the Yaquis,
And freely risk their hard-earned tlacos
In games of chance and sports and races,
Just as they do in other places;
"All the world's a stage," as Shakespeare says,
And where's the man but sometimes plays?

A bull-fight may be seen in Spain.
In Cuba, or on the Spanish Main;
But here, to make the sport more rare,
We matched a bull against a bear.
The horse-corral formed ample theater,
The walls around formed amphitheater,
Where guests in safety watched the sight
Of bull and bruin come to fight.
After sundry passes, thrusts, and turns,
The bull tossed bruin on his horns.

Our nights were spent in Spanish dancing,
And when the night was found advancing,
We passed around the loving cup,
To keep the dancers' spirits up.
To make this cup is quite a secret,
But as you're a man, of course you'll keep it:
Rum, brandy, or whisky makes the body,
And for a flavor, apple-toddy,
Champagne frappé, and rich ice-cream—
To bed, and of the angels dream.

The night before the year expires,
We improvise a night surprise,
To leave on memory pleasant phantoms.
The lake was covered with Chinese lanterns,
Each strung on wire, which moved about,
As the Chinese pulled them in and out,
In shape of mimic ships on fire,
And grotesque imps on dancing wire;
A pyrotechnical display
Gives welcome to the New Year's day.

TUBAC & THE SANTA RITA Mts from the S.E. side.

An emperor, in days of yore,
Sought daughter lost along the shore,
With lanterns, boats, and dredging gear,
For she was drowned, they all did fear.
By lighting all the lake around,
The father soon his daughter found;
And in gratitude to great Shang-té,
Made laws that always, on the sea,
The feast of lanterns should be kept,
For daughter found, who erst was wept.

Our guests were gone;
We three alone
The Winter days and nights must pass,
Secluded now and lone. Alas,
That, from the ark let loose, the dove
Found olive-branch to bear above!
The family have since dispersed,
And those most thoroughly well versed
In lineage can't trace their tree,
As it has spread o'er land and sea.

We watched the sunrise day by day,
In morning dawn with silver ray,
Send forth through Santa Rita's peaks
His first clear-pointed silver streaks;
By noon he rolled, a copper god,
O'er mountain peaks by man ne'er trod;
At evening, gold, with purple clouds,
Majestic, gorgeous, golden shrouds;
He sinks beyond Babaquivari,
To rest in far Pacific sea.

My father strung the soft guitar,
My mother sung some Moorish air;
The zithern melted in her hand,
As she played and sung of Moorish land.
My Pima maid and I kept tune.
These Indians have a vocal boon;
They sing with melody and heart,
And could excel in vocal art;
The climate favors voice and lung,
And this is the very land of song.

In spring the mountain torrents loosed
Some flakes of gold from craggy roost,
And brought them down the grand canal,
Which flowed along our peaceful val.
The Eden serpent come by stealth!
Oh, false, vain counterfeit of wealth!
Oh, cursed gold, oh, fiendish dross!
Your fancied gain was our great loss.
They fascinated father's eyes,
And he gave up all to win the prize.

No more the land was tilled for bread,
No more at night the Bible read.
No more was wife or child cared for;
The only deity now was d'or.
For machines of heavy bulk and weight,
My father pledged the vast estate
To Tubac's chief, who dealt in ores,
And furnished miners mining stores;
His Spanish nature all soon changed,
And from his family estranged.

All love and courtesy now denied,
My gentle mother pined and died;
The first spring violets on her grave,
A prayer to Mary her soul to save ;
A child brought up in Moorish bowers,
Who watched the sea from father's towers,
Here buried in these western mountains,
It brings the tears from driest fountains ;
This was the first sincere youth's sorrow
Which forever clouds life's coming morrow.

One Sabbath morn, at break of day,
When counting mother's rosary,
A cry rang out so wild and high,
That it had almost pierced the sky—
Apaches ! that dreadful knell,
Announcing here these fiends of hell;
Apaches ! ! that dreadful note,
That makes the breath stick in the throat ;
Apaches ! ! ! that dreadful doom,
That shadowed forth a bloody tomb.

The savages prepared at night
To make attack at dawn of light;
My father fell at his own door,
Filling the " salvatum " sill with gore;
A red fiend caught me round the waist,
And on my father's best horse placed;
Then mounting on behind, gave lash,
And passed away, like lightning flash.
My Pima maid swung by the hair,
In gripe of other savage bear.

About a hundred rode behind,
With spoil of horses and of kine.
We passed Sopori in two hours—
The smoke was issuing from the towers;
There was no sign of cow nor horse—
Old Douglass lay a bloody corse,
With neither friend nor kinsman near,
To perform the rites of sepulture;
His faithful harpers beside him lay,
And requiem played as they passed away.

By noon we crossed the Santa Cruz.
Oh! holy name of Cross, infuse
Some pity in the saints above,
To rescue me, for Christ's dear love.
Oh! for some power divine, alack!
To telegraph to old Tubac;
The chief would gather all his clan,
And make pursuit becoming man;
For nothing so becomes the brave,
As weak and captured maid to save.

At evening, as the setting sun
Threw its last lingering beams upon
The towers and domes of San Xavier,
We passed in sight and very near
Where pious priests, and nuns among,
Chanted the wonted vesper-song.
Oh! holy Mary, pity have,
And a lost and helpless maiden save.
I struggled in my captor's vice,
And threw a kiss to the cross of Christ.

Oh! for a magic telephone
To communicate with old Tucson;
Her chivalry would quickly arm,
And never let me come to harm.
The Oury's brave as lion's cubs,
And dare-devil as Beelzebubs;
Pete Kitchen on his skew-bald horse,
With Papago auxiliary force,
Would make pursuit with bated breath,
To rescue, or to meet their death.

The night came on, we thundered on;
All hope of rescue now was gone.
We scoured across the plain,
The livelong night ne'er drew a rein.
I tore some slips from my night-gown,
And slyly dropped them on the ground
To guide pursuit, if any came.
I bowed my head to the horse's mane,
And prayed the orphan's only Friend
Relief and succor soon to send.

At dawn of day on Gila's banks
Our caballada cooled their flanks,
And rested here for rise of sun.
The Apache's northern goal was won;
For Gila forms the boundary line
Between these nomads and mankind.
Towards the east the Rio Grande
Forms eastern boundary of their land;
The Colorado's stream runs by
The golden rim of their western sky.

While beasts rushed down to water's edge
Their burning thirst to there assuage,
The Indians hastened to prepare
The rudest kind of hunter's fare;
Fat burro steaks, and roast maguey,
With pachete, and with mesquite tea;
Then washed themselves in Gila's flood,
To clear away the stains of blood;
For Apaches all from food refrain
Till hands are freed from bloody stain.

A watch was set upon a rise,
To guard the camp against surprise,
And Gila's rugged cañon made
A strong and natural ambuscade
To trap pursuers from the south,
While others drove the cattle north;
The trail wound round by Saddle Peak,
And followed up Aliso Creek
To where San Carlos' waters gleam
And form a junction with the stream.

Another night was passed in travel,
O'er bowlders, rocks, and sand and gravel;
When morning's sun, o'er mountain broke,
Revealed the blue Apache smoke
Arising from the rock Cañada,
Which guards their camp and caballada
In horseshoe shape, the heel at mouth,
Egress and entrance from the south,
Where about a thousand Indians dwelt,
Who never fear nor danger felt.

ANCIENT CLIFF HOUSE.

The camp, aroused by watchful scouts,
Received their braves with welcome shouts;
Made fair division of the spoil,
Without contention rude, or broil,
Each taking fair and just proportion,
As he had furnished contribution,
Or personally efforts made
In consummation of the raid.
But what a mental agony
To know what should become of me!

The captors were a Pinal band,
Who occupy this mountain land;
The Gila River on the south,
The mountain ranges to the north,
Rising in range o'er range so high,
The topmost range shuts out the sky;
The Rio Verde binds the west,
The Rio Grande towards the east;
The central river, called the Salt,
Runs through deep cañons of basalt.

The chief was Mangus Colorado,
A great, stern chief, without bravado—
"Red Sleeve," in English patronymic;
He gained this name, in barbarous mimic,
For deeds of savage hardihood,
Which covered his right arm with blood.
My captor was his son Cachise,
A chief more famed for war than peace.
These Indians from their captives learn
Many a useful art and turn.

The old chief took my hand and spoke
In Spanish, with Indian gutturals broke:
"Young maiden, do not shake your hands.
Your captors are not Mexicans,
But men who always spare the brave,
The virtue of their captives save.
Descended from the Mongol race,
These mountains form our resting-place;
The ancient chieftains of our clan
Were Tamerlane and Ghenghis Khan.

"With Asian conquests not content,
We came to take this continent,
And founded here, at old Tubac,
The empire old of Anahuac.
The Spaniard came, with thirst for gold,
With novel arms, that thunder rolled,
And drove us from the plains below—
Overmatches for our lance and bow;
We'll ne'er forgive their mongrel brood,
Until we wipe it out in blood.

"But you, a woman, rest content,
And share my wife and daughter's tent.
The laws of Tartar clans forbid
Their sons with captive maids to wed;
While race of Tooglook's sons endure,
Their blood and lineage must be pure.
Your menial service will suffice
For this domestic sacrifice;
You can my daughter teach the arts
Which you have learned in foreign parts.

"Our women famed for chastity
As ermine of Alaska's sea,
That cannot bear the slighest blurr
Upon their snow-white vesture pure.
Your mongrel race cut off the hair
From women caught in vice's lair;
But we, more rigid, mark the face
So time nor art cannot efface;
The punishment we have for those,
Is amputation of the nose."

The tents were formed of willow poles
Set round in circles, stuck in holes,
The tops made to the center meet,
A rustic dome 'gainst rain and sleet,
With covering of brush and hides,
And skins of beasts to line the sides.
Thus nature teaches savage men
First principles of art to ken,
First lesson in architecture given
From model of the dome of heaven.

The morning duty first begins
With filling all the water-skins,
Which, made of leather and rawhide,
With thongs of deer securely tied,
Contain the water for the day,
And hang convenient for foray;
These leathern botas, not ornate,
The heated vapour exhalate,
And keep the water fresh and cool
As mountain spring or icy pool.

The firewood, next, was gathered in.
A bullock's rawhide formed the bin,
The fore-legs looped around our necks,
The hind-legs stretched on forked sticks.
The loads, filled in with mesquite limbs
And branches that the Apache trims,
With bark of oak and cottonwood,
And others that for fires are good,
Formed burden of such heavy ponder
That we could scarcely stagger under.

The morning meal prepared in haste,
Of bullock's steaks and mesquite paste,
We commenced the labors of the day,
The hides of savage beasts to fray;
They first were soaked in water-lime,
Subjected then a while to brine,
The hair to loosen and make soft,
So we could easily rub it off
With polished drawing knives of ash,
Which soon made skins as soft as sash.

In season when the plant maguey
Gives flower to bloom its scent away
On desert air, in place remote—
A plant about which Chinese wrote;
They called the aloe-plant "Fusang,"
And Oriental praises sang
Two thousand years and more ago,
To fruit and flower of aloe—
A food for either man or beast;
A spirit giving divine surcease.

This aloe grows on mountain-sides,
In desert lands its beauty hides,
And yields to man its saccharine bread,
About the size of cabbage-head;
The head is cut and shorn of thorn
And flower which its top adorn,
Then placed in oven, underground,
And roasted till its meat is found—
The substitute Apache bread,
Which nature forms from maguey-head.

The men another custom have—
The leaves of maguey-head they shave,
Then mash the substance to a pulp,
Compressing all the juice of bulb
Into a vat of stout rawhides,
From which the sun the juice oxides,
Forming a simple fermentation,
Producing Apache intoxication.
This liquor, distilled in horns alembous,
Causes a "delirium tremendous."

The Tizween drink is much enjoyed;
To make it Indian corn's employed;
They bury the corn until it sprouts—
Destroying food for drinking bouts;
Then grind it in a kind of tray,
Then boil it strong about a day;
Strain off the juice in willow sieve,
And in the sun to ferment leave.
The fermented juice is called tulpai,
On which Apache chief gets high.

The oak majestic yields her quota,
The fruit of which is called bellota.
Gathered and stored for winter's use,
To give nutrition and amuse.
At eve, around the wild camp-fire,
The roasted acorn serves to tire
The tedium of night away;
And in Apache fun and play,
The vulgar gouber's superseded,
And manners to the old are heeded.

Beside the fruits of the wild cherry,
The manzanita bears a berry,
From which an acid drink is made,
And called a mountain lemonade;
The wild-pea gives its imitation
In this wild desert vegetation,
And furnishes, preserved in pod,
Another evidence that God,
In wilderness howe'er remote,
Provides some food for man's support.

You're not so ignorant, I hope,
To think that Indians ne'er use soap,
When nature spreads it in their way,
Abundant as the soft maguey.
The yucca seeds form an atole,
The root's a saponaceous amole,
Which maids and matrons freely gather,
To make a serviceable lather
To cleanse the skin as clean as snow,
And make the hair and pechos grow.

The women gather willow boughs,
Which grow where'er the water flows,
And cutting off the limbs and leaves,
A strong and useful basket weaves,
Which, tightly glued with gum mesquite,
With painted figures strange and neat,
Makes utensil which for use and looks
Might well be used by better folks.
The first domestic willow use
Is to cradle small Apach' papoose.

The men engaged in manly games,
With wild, uncouth Apache names;
The ball of stone on horse to roll
With long and polished maguey pole.
A hole drilled half-way through the rock,
Gave point of vantage for the shock,
Which skillful rider strove to win
By driving pole the hole within,
Then riding with stone poised on high,
As evidence of victory.

The race-course, formed by nature's hand
Where rough sierras bound the land,
Gave ample space for coursers fleet,
Their match in strength and speed to meet;
The Apache scorns the barbed bit,
And fashions bridle far more fit,
Of rawhide round the lower jaw,
With reins of hair the horse to draw;
Then mounting bareback on the steed,
He puts him to his greatest speed.

To shoe a horse in fashion coarse,
The Apache never hurts a horse;
The smithy gently takes his foot,
And fastens on a rawhide boot,
Which, strapped the ankle-joint above,
Makes fit as tight as lady's glove;
The hide put on is soft and wet,
To make a neat and perfect set,
Then left in sun his hoof to dry on,
Makes shoe as good and hard as iron.

In games of cards the men delight,
And over monte often fight.
The cards are made of hardened leather,
Defying time, and use, and weather;
A greasy pack, with painted kings,
And queens, and jacks, and all such things,
As sportsmen typify the game,
And ladies scarcely know the name—
A sport confined to men's diversion,
To which the women have aversion.

The rules adopted for the dance
Exceed the politesse of France;
The young bucks form a ring around,
The maids are placed in center ground;
And when the music from tom-tom,
Accompanied by rawhide drum,
Arouses itching of the toes,
Each maiden for her favorite goes,
Evincing thus her fond affection,
And making natural selection.

Each state has its Eleusinian games,
To grace events that have no names.
They here prepare a festive race
For girl arrived at woman's place,
And strew the course with flowers round,
And spread their presents on the ground.
The girl, with others more mature,
Tries what her pubert strength can endure.
The flowers and gifts, caught by the way,
Are ornaments for wedding-day.

The summer passed in sport and frolic,
The Apaches ne'er get melancholic.
The autumn fruits were stored away,
With stacks of juicy roast maguey;
The skins were full of roast bellotas,
And mescal juice filled up the botas;
The costals filled with pemmican,
And strong meats for the wants of man.
The summer heats have passed away,
And autumn bids a fierce foray.

The Apache thinks the husbandman
A peon, who only tills the land
For use of lords of nomad race,
Who scorn to earn, by sweat of face,
The bread to feed their little ones,
Or clothes to clothe their pretty ones,
And follows out the good old plan
Of get who may and keep who can;
That herders are but Ishmaelites,
To fatten those who win the fights.

The country south a hundred leagues
Was full of corn and wine and trigos,
Fat cattle, horses, mules, and pelf—
Enough to tempt old Nick himself.
The natives robbed them of their land,
Made them a nomad robber band.
Why should they not retaliate,
And ravage, murder, vengeance sate,
Upon the dirty mongrel race
Who occupy the Spaniard's place?

The leader of the first foray,
A young chief named Pion-Senay,
Who called for braves to join his band,
For raid upon Sonora land.
They came in numbers thick and fast,
Each eager not to be the last;
Their horses fat and sleek with feed,
Their arms prepared for time of need,
Their lances polished bright as steel,
They sallied forth to rob and steal.

The new moon pointed to the south,
Its horns erect, presaging drouth;
For, like all nomads planning rides,
They take the planets for their guides.
A scanty ration served their use;
A leathern flask of mescal juice,
A buckskin bag of ground pañole—
For sustenance this formed the whole;
For warriors going on the scent,
Go free of all impediment.

A full moon generally suffices,
Gives time enough to gain their prizes;
They march at night, and in the day
From mountain tops the roads waylay.
The ranchers gather herds and flocks
In corrals built of adobes or rocks;
The Apaches steal around the pens,
And stealthily, to gain their ends,
Saw doors in mud with stout hair rope,
And with the caballada elope.

If cunning ranchmen interpose
Some sticks or stones in building close,
So Apache saw can make no way,
They undertake another way;
The ropes are fastened on the walls,
The Apaches mount into corrals;
Each singling out the fleetest horse,
They await the break of day, of course,
When sleepy ranchmen drop the bars,
And scarcely can believe their stars,
When Apaches, with a loud hurrah,
Before them drive their herds afar.

The ranchmen seldom make pursuit,
Admonished by its bitter fruit;
The Apaches, watching in the rear,
Descry a dust in atmosphere,
Dispatch the booty on ahead;
An ambuscade is quickly made
Behind a ledge of rocks on road,
Or by the river's bank or ford.
Pursuers always come to grief,
And get far more of lead than beef.

The moon was waning in the east,
The time had come for Apache feast,
When just about the break of day
The scouts announced Pion-Senay;
Three hundred head of stock he drove
For shelter, in our wild alcove,
And loads of corn, and wheat, and beans,
Were added to our winter means;
With stuffs and goods for winter dresses,
And ornaments to bind our tresses.

The news, brought in by raiding band,
Caused great stir in Apache-land;
Another flag now floats the breeze,
And waves above the cottonwood trees.
The flag that carrion-buzzard flaws,
With hated nopal in his claws,
Is furled and silently withdrawn.
Another flag floats o'er Tucson;
The eagle soars 'midst countless stars,
The king of birds in peace or wars.

The flag unfurled on Bunker Hill
Has come, the emblem of good-will,
A thousand leagues, or thereabouts.
This starry banner waves and floats,
Flag of the brave, flag of the free—
It may give liberty to me.
They told of horsemen in blue coats,
And wild, resounding bugle notes;
And cannon thundering o'er the plain,
And guns that fired, and fired again.

The brave Cachise led next foray,
The largest raid for many a day.
A hundred horsemen sallied out,
Armed for the battle and the rout;
The moon scarce waned on Pinal hills,
When wails the Apache valley fills;
Cachise alone, of all his band,
Comes wounded to Apache-land.
The clan soon gathered in the vale,
To hear the wounded warrior's tale.

He said: "I led the wonted trails
To where the running water fails,
And rushes back upon the sands
Like coursers of Apache bands,
Unfit for use of man or beast,
So salty to the smell and taste.
We gathered on the Yaqui, sheep,
And left the herders in the sleep
Which sent their spirits gathering wool,
Where fleecy clouds above us roll.

"A band of horses, next, we planned,
Bearing the Alamitta brand;
The herders made a brave defense,
And many felt Apache lance;
The rest were tied with running noose,
Made of their own rawhide lassos,
Around the neck, and left to stretch
Their limbs above the water-ditch,
On limbs of lofty alamos,
Which on the Alamitta grows.

"A herd of cattle, next, were seen,
 Upon the Noria Verde green;
 Estrella's brand their flanks defaced.
 The vaqueros one another raced,
 In haste to gain their torreon,
 While we drove all the cattle on.
 We passed the ruined Aribac,
 Where not a human being's track
 Remains to mark the former state
 Of life upon this grand estate.

"The Sopori towers in ruins tumble,
 The walls of Douglass ruined crumble,
 And none remain to work the mine,
 Or plant the field, or tend the kine.
 We crossed the Santa Cruz at noon,
 Half-way from Tubac to Tucson,
 And made a camp upon the creek,
 Just north of Santa Rita's peak,
 Where grama grass and woods abound,
 And rest from our long drive was found.

"We turned the cattle out to graze,
 And made our meal of Indian maize,
 Then stretched us out to seek repose
 Beneath the quercus' shady boughs,
 When, like a thunder-clap upon
 The camp, crashed the repeating-gun;
 With steady fire of rifle-ball
 And pistol-shot, my men all fall,
 Dragoons in blue the camp surround,
 And in a moment I am bound.

VALLEY of SANTA CRUZ

"My few surviving braves were hung
 On trees, to make the ravens' dung,
 And I, in thongs of stout rawhide,
 Was led the captain's tent beside;
 He said, wide pointing with his hands:
'This land no more is Mexican's;
 We bought it from the dirty race,
 And come in power to take our place;
 To spread our flag from mountain-top,
 To guard the roads, and foray stop.

"'Your race forever, from henceforth,
 Must keep yourselves in mountains north;
 The Gila's ford on south must be
 Henceforth, your utmost boundary;
 And each Apache across this bound,
 In arms or stealth hereafter found,
 Shall suffer death by rifle ball.
 Or, if as captive he should fall,
 He shall be hanged upon a tree,
 As warning sign of infamy.'

"My Tartar blood boiled as he spoke;
 As soon as I my gorge could choke,
 I answered: 'This is not your land,
 And ne'er belonged to Mexican.
 We owned this land long years ago,
 From where the mountain rivers flow
 To shores of the vermilion sea.
 Our sires have always roamed it free,
 And we for it will bravely die,
 Before we'll to the mountains fly.

"'These lands were ours in nature's fee,
  Before you whites e'er crossed the sea.
  Go back and leave us here alone;
  Take warning now, and quick be gone.
  Our clans are countless in the north,
  And vengeful soon will issue forth
  To murder, rob, waylay the roads,
  And ambuscade the river fords.
  We cannot live in mountain pens;
  Go back, and let us yet be friends.'

"The haughty captain got in rage—
  For he was somewhat under age—
  Bascomb by name—he drew his sword,
  And without saying another word,
  In angry manner, most uncouth,
  Struck me a blow upon the mouth.
  The sentinel led me away
  To guarded tent, at close of day,
  In silent darkness there to brood
  On plans of vengeance and of blood.

"I sat amid the sighing trees,
  And bowed my head upon my knees,
  And knit my hands into my cue,
  Where a butcher-knife was hid from view.
  With this I quickly cut my thongs,
  And straight prepared to right my wrongs;
  The guardsman shuddered with a start
  As I plunged the knife into his heart;
  Then, mounting horse at picket-post,
  Cachise was soon to vision lost."

Soon as Cachise had told his tale,
The tribe commenced a mournful wail.
A hundred braves, or ninety-nine,
Were sadly missed in battle line.
The young could scarcely bend the bow,
The old were too infirm to go;
The women, now fresh-widowed wives,
Began to whet the butcher knives.
Old Mangus rose upon his spear,
Commanding all around to hear.

"My son," he said, "my life is sped,
No more can braves by me be led.
In youthful days my lance drank gore
From Mexicans, and cried for more;
A treacherous and a thieving race,
In whom kind pity finds no place.
Now these Americans have come
In numbers strong, to seal our doom;
But fight them while a soul survives,
Fight for our homes, our sons, our wives,

"Go! light the fires on mountain peaks,
And tell the chiefs old Mangus speaks;
In tongue of flame, the war proclaim,
And from each clan its fealty claim;
Spread far and wide the war fire-brand,
From Colorado to Rio Grande;
Make treaty with the Mescaleros,
And band with us the Coyoteros;
Bid Alexandro join our band,
And bring with him his brave command.

"Go! tell the brave Eskiminzin
  To come and join the battle's din;
  Give notice to Mimbreños bold,
  To watch upon the cañon's hold,
  To ambuscade the road's approaches,
  And rob the overland mail-coaches;
  The Tonto chief, old Delashay,
  Must guard the pass's western way,
  And from the Casablanca's mounds
  Must keep the Pimas within bounds.

"Send message to Qua-shack-a-ma,
  The Yavapai chief, to join the war,
  And even let them go as far
  As Chemihuevis Espanquya;
  The wily scoundrel may assist us,
  If we would dearly buy his sisters;
  The Mohaves, Yumas, Cocopas,
  Are lost to sense of honor's laws,
  And since the trade in gold began,
  Are panders to the American.

" The Navajos are brave and good;
  In former days they battle stood;
  With lance in rest and horse array,
  They led the first in wild foray;
  But now they're fed on beef and beans,
  Poor paupers on the stranger's means;
  Reduced to vassalage and fear,
  They dare not face the pale face here,
  Although our blood is still the same,
  For they have only changed their name.

"It boots us not who comes or goes;
We'll fight to death our nation's foes.
Our tribe is twenty thousand strong,
Men and women, old and young.
The war-cloud gathers o'er my race;
I go from hence to mount my place;
My race is run, my end has come.
In superstition's mountain dome,
My spirit watches o'er the fray,
And waits the break of eternal day."

Ten years the war raged far and wide,
With advantage on the Apache side;
And in this time bold deeds were done,
Which would have honored Priam's son.
No Homer sings Apache praise;
No bard perpetuates their lays.
The white man's pen, with printer's ink,
Exalted deeds which fairly stink.
The prince of knaves, and liars, and cowards,
Was named the last of all the Howards.

The braves were out upon the scout,
The meal was thin, the meat was out;
The winter passed in dismal gloom;
Starvation seemed to be our doom.
The spring came on—the blessed spring,
Which genial blessings ought to bring;
But here no cheerful sounds at morn,
No men remain to plant the corn;
The women wail their husbands lost;
Who go to war should count the cost.

Our means of living all were spent;
My Pima maid and I were sent
To strip the willows of their leaves,
And bind them up in handy sheaves;
To strip the bark from off the tree,
And boil it for Apache tea.
The pulp, when beaten to a shred,
Was made in cakes, for Apache bread.
So great our hunger came at last,
That life was a continual fast.

We hid the boughs away by stealth,
As miser hoards his hidden wealth,
And in the day commenced to weave
A willow boat in which to leave;
For only thus was any hope
With Apache vigilance to cope.
For any track upon the land,
Would sure betray us to the band,
Who soon our hiding-place would find;
But water leaves no tracks behind.

My former knowledge of the sea
Was now the stead of life to me;
We laid the keel of willow pole,
Then bent the bough around the hold,
And firmly bound our tiny ark
With pliant strips of willow bark;
Then caulked the bottom tight and neat,
From stem to stern with gum mesquite;
And when our boat the river struck,
She sat the water like a duck.

We launched her on the broad Salado,
As night began to cast its shadow;
And guided her among the shoals,
With willing hands and willow poles.
All night the river thundered on,
In narrow gorge and deep cañon;
Its rocky banks sometimes so high,
That precipice shut out the sky.
The rapids were so steep and narrow,
The boat shot through them like an arrow.

With speed so swift by break of day,
The Apache camp was far away;
The sun first sent its silver streaks,
Astern, above the Chromo peaks.
At noon we stopped, a rest to seek,
In debouchure of Tonto creek,
And sought our hunger to appease
By eating bark from off the trees;
Of willow twigs we made a net,
And sylvan snare for fish was set.

The mountain trout are very shy,
But, tying in the net a fly,
They dived, their appetite to gloat,
And next were floundering in the boat.
Let captious epicures decide
If fish are better boiled or fried;
But others from experience draw
Conclusion that they 're better raw;
For Oriental travelers know
The Japanese all eat them so.

The sun aslant his evening streaks
Was shedding westward of Four Peaks,
When, following his golden beam,
We launched our boat into the stream,
And soon again the light of day
Was lost to us in perils' way.
The cañons high, stupendous sides
The very stars obscure and hide;
A night of such tremendous horror,
We thought we ne'er should see the morrow.

The boat threw foam upon her tracks,
And danced along the cataracts;
Then caught up in the whirlpool's swirl,
Spun round and round in giddy whirl,
Till I and my poor Pima girl
Thought we had parted with the world.
But God above our lives ordains;
To change the plan is wrong and vain.
'Tis all the same, on sea or land—
We're in the hollow of his hand.

The last chute through a mountain-chain
Revealed to westward, verdant plain,
Where mountains, far as eye could see,
Rose up like islands from the sea.
In the cañon we but saw the moon,
And on the plain the sun marked noon.
Enchanted river, fare thee well,
Your gates are like the jaws of hell.
The porphyry columns tower on high,
Mute sentinels against the sky.

We drifted gently down the stream,
And soon my soul began to dream
Of childhood's Andalusian bowers,
And scented, perfumed Cuban flowers;
Was rocked upon the Spanish Main,
The Chinese music heard again;
Was waltzing, home at Arivac,
In arms of chief of old Tubac;
And on my satin pillow lay,
And dreamed and dreamed of wedding-day.

A gentle touch upon my head,
My Pima maiden gently said:
"See there, a smoke upon the plain;
We now shall meet our friends again.
The Pimas burn away the brush,
To plant against the river's flush;
They here mayhap may have some seed,
To serve us in our utmost need.
Our lives are safe, our freedom won,
Let's kneel and glorify the sun."

Again I dozed off in a dream.
The Pimas waded in the stream
To where the poppies' flowerets float,
And gently carried out the boat;
They lashed some poles unto the sides,
And marched away with giant strides.
I thought again I was on horse,
And scouring o'er the Apache course,
The Indians following on the plain;
The sun had nearly baked my brain.

The Pimas took us in their hands,
Like good and kind Samaritans;
Fed us with dainty chicken broth,
And gave us clothes of cotton cloth,
Of fiber woven by their hands,
From cotton raised upon their lands.
Old Anton Azul, the chief, was dead,
His children knocked him in the head;
A custom Pima Indians have,
When decrepit age should seek the grave.

If ills afflict a male adult,
They call in men of skill occult;
But woe to doctor if patient dies—
His physician tends him to the skies;
The dead are buried in the ground,
And form the bulk of Pima Mound;
Their souls around the village stop,
To tend the herds and watch the crop;
The Pima spirits disenthralled,
In Pima tongue are "quetties" called.

The Pima maids, like angel sisters,
In every way tried to assist us,
To make our clothes, to comely dress,
And help us soon to convalesce.
The Willow Leaf, Hah-wul-hahake,
Made me her bed and board partake;
Heosick Nunea, the Flower Singing,
Was always some little dainty bringing;
The Branching Flower, Mamelot Heosick,
Was nightingale among the sick.

Nea Volpusz, the Running Song,
Was never absent from us long;
The Leaf-Wind, Hahak Hersoul,
Of mirth and laughter was the soul;
And Moi-eol, Nightshade, Belladonna,
Proved woman was the soul of honor;
Oral, Nishit, and Frothy Waters,
Were Pima matron's well-trained daughters;
The Singing Flower, Nea Heosick,
Was Pine Flower's cousin, Hook Heosick.

Vek Heosick, the Feathered Flower,
Had beauty for her native dower,
And Feather Tassel, Vek Molet,
Was dark blue like the violet;
The Shady Leaf, Tonel Hahake,
Helped others to sweet music make.
The Pima voice is soft and sweet,
The words in songs they oft repeat;
The instruments their skill affords,
Are made of horsehairs strung on gourds.

The Plum-like Damsel, Vek-e-mos,
Had plum-like cheeks as soft as moss;
The Snowy Leaves, Young Le Hahok,
And Che-hea-pik, the Corral Smoke,
See-áá-ke-mul, the Moving Rivers,
Who made the arrows for the quivers;
The Bounding Cloud, Cheorak Womoekuf,
Makes nearly Pima names enough;
Though Bow Flower, Kat Heosick, and Cliff Waters,
Varu Susook, are Pima daughters.

While men deal with affairs of state,
Each girl's allowed to choose her mate;
If nature's charms fail to inspire
The burning flame of love's desire,
A candidate whose passed her teens
Resorts to artificial means,
And makes love-powder of a flower—
"Flor de la tierra," which has the power
The wildest buck to fascinate,
And bind in the connubial state.

The courtship shy 'twixt boy and lass
Is carried on with looking-glass;
With wonderful finesse and tact,
They seat themselves down back to back;
And gesture love in dumb emotion,
To manifest their fond devotion.
By smiles and amatory glances,
Each suitor may divine his chances;
And when the maid gives him the pass,
She blows her breath upon the glass.

If philter, glass, and opiate
Fail to secure congenial mate,
The Pimas never seek resort
In law's divorce or aid of court;
Never obtrude domestic strife,
Nor give to ridicule the wife;
But terminate the social bother
By making bargains with each other;
To neighbor's wife the question pop,
And make a neat domestic swap.

I lingered here a month or more,
To wasted health and strength restore;
When preparations were begun,
To go on homewards by Tucson;
If home indeed the world contains
For orphan maid from captive chains.
The Pimas rigged my willow boat
As palanquin, themselves to tote,
With serapé of cotton spun,
For canopy against the sun.

My Pima maid I bade farewell,
Among her kindred here to dwell,
Where peace and plenty from the land
Kind nature gives with lavish hand.
If happiness on earth there be,
Those Pimas find it *sans souci*.
They worship as a god the sun,
As his diurnal courses run.
Without a thought, without a care,
Content and peace are resting here.

A hundred horsemen, armed with lance,
Half in rear and half advance,
Formed escort from Apache raid,
And guarded home the rescued maid.
The starry flag was high out thrown,
From plaza staff of old Tucson;
The gallants met us on the road,
And sweet bouquets on us bestowed;
The welcome's loud resound was rung,
As on Christian land again I sprung.

A day of rest and gen'rous cheer,
We then move on to San Xavier,
Where holy father holds a mass,
And sends me message not to pass,
But stop and render thanks to God,
And worship at my mother's sod.
These duties done, at rise of sun
Next day, the journey home begun,
And evening sun's rich golden streaks
Were gilding Babaquivera's peaks.

His last reflected glimmering sheen
Was laid on Arivaca's green;
The bonfires lighted up the towers,
The fountain played upon the flowers,
When Tubac's chief, in evening dress,
Stood at the door, with all his mess,
In accents cordial, kind, and grave,
A hospitable welcome gave
At very spot in corridor,
Which I'll recall forevermore.

"This place is mine by law and right;
By courtesy, 'tis yours to-night.
From here you nevermore shall roam;
Stay here with me; adorn this home;
And while I have a crust of bread,
You shall have where to lay your head.
Go change your dress; your room's prepared,
Your toilet spread, your clothes well aired;
Be quick, no longer tempt the fates;
You must be hungry; dinner waits."

The Tubac chief now holds the reins,
And works among the silver veins,
With steam machines of pond'rous weights,
And tools imported from the States.
His German staff know how to mine,
From education on the Rhine;
Their science, skill, and shrewd design
With native labor here combine,
And in this far-off wilderness
Make silver mines a great success.

Strange, pensive man, what brought him here?
A spirit mild thrown out of sphere.
'Twas not for gold he sought this land—
He scatters that with lavish hand.
For honor? No—from that exempt,
He bears mankind too much contempt.
It must be some domestic woe.
If this be true, then leave it so;
A woman's mission on this globe
Is wounds to soothe—not wounds to probe.

I know not, care not, what it be,
I know he's all the world to me.
I ask no grace from God nor man,
The soul is free, love where it can.
No priestly hands can give it ease,
Much less a justice of the peace.
The world and I are far apart,
I have no guide but my own heart.
This mentor swells within my breast,
And softens when I am caressed.

The days and weeks and months passed on,
The memory of sorrow 's gone.
The lotus leaves formed all our food,
We spent the time in doing good.
No man applied for work in vain,
No woman left alone in pain;
The country 'round for a hundred miles
Was clad in fortune's prosperous smiles;
The engines thundered night and day,
In grinding ores of richest ley.

A little music now and then,
At eve a gallop on the plain.
My mare, as white as driven snow,
Was trained in canter fast to go.
With riding-dress and snow-white plume,
My health again began to bloom.
My chief bestrode a coal-black steed
Of famous rancher Maxwell's breed.
"Tempest" and "Sunshine," names devised
To typify our checkered lives.

A year passed by as but a day,
The flowers began to bloom in May;
My garden occupied my time,
My chief was busy with the mine;
One day in June, with clouded brow
A rare occurrence with him now—
An official paper in his hand,
Sent by the captain, in command
Of Fort Buchanan, rueful name,
Forever linked to nation's shame.

"My dear," he said, "this paper says
  Some things that soon must part our ways;
  The war-cloud bursting in the south,
  Has brought its direful vengeance forth.
  Old Twiggs surrendered his command
  In Texas, to the rebel band;
  And Lynde, upon the Rio Grande,
  Has made his gallant troops disband.
  The flag in which we put our trust,
  Dishonored now, trails in the dust.

"This order here, alas! proclaims,
  This country must be given to flames,
  And nothing left upon the land,
  From Colorado to Rio Grande,
  Which can an enemy maintain,
  Or let them food or aid obtain.
  They fear a California raid,
  And order the road a desert made;
  The troops march out with shotted gun,
  The flag first meets the eastern sun.

"I cannot hold against the tide
  And clash of arms on every side;
  The Apaches will be down from north,
  And robber Mexicans from south.
  The people hear the battle cry,
  And from this waste begin to fly.
  One hope remains, and only one,
  And for this you must soon be gone.
  'Tis imperative that you should go
  To work our plans in Mexico.

"See Maxmilian; bribe Bazaine;
Join the good Carlotta's train.
For full ten million francs take bills;
The bank of France our silver fills.
Spread presents out with lavish hand,
Strain every nerve to hold our land.
Tell Maxmilian, one command
Can hold the pass of Rio Grande;
To Guaymas let him send gunboats,
And here the flag of empire floats.

"Good Hulsemann shall go with you;
He's always been most kind and true,
Speaks every tongue beneath the sun,
And of my staff's the chosen one.
Your beauty, since I've won the prize,
May go to dazzle other eyes.
Your heart, firm locked in my embrace,
Will scarcely seek another place.
The 'tempest' past, 'sunshine' again,
We'll canter lightly o'er the plain."

We parted at the corridor;
Oh! when shall we two meet once more?
That, God himself alone can tell;
I go to do my duty well.
From Guaymas' port to Mazatlan
We sailed in vessel contraband.
From here, through land of fair Valencia,
We passed in country dilijencia,
To where the mountain water falls
Round Montezuma's ruined halls.

Great Cortez found an empire here,
On continent without a peer.
The Spaniards ruled with iron rod,
And taught with lash the love of God.
The natives, lashed to desperation,
In vain have tried to make a nation;
Their vengeful natures spill the blood
Of all who try to do them good.
First Iturbide's blood was spilled,
And Indians seize the place he filled.

Burr's scheme, the next, was well designed—
Ambition almost unconfined.
But factions rampant in the state,
Forbid this should be consummate.
The English then, to break Spain's power,
Watched every point, and seized the hour
Of America's weakest President;
A diplomatic message sent,
And Canning's cunning doctrine goes
Down history's gullet as Monroe's.

The piebald nations which proclaim
"Republic"—only so in name—
Are natural offspring of the trick
Which royalty imposed so slick
On Uncle Sam, then but a boy,
And tickled with his new-found toy.
This hybrid race are like their mules—
Begot in breach of nature's rules;
Which God forbids to leave a trace,
By getting others of their race.

The great Scott came with fuss and feathers;
In Montezuma's halls he tethers,
And had not very long been there,
When he cries, "Help, to let go this bear."
The Sphinx of France, next, looked afar,
To guard against domestic war,
And give the chivalry of France,
At Mexico, a little chance;
But figurehead for this emprise,
Must noble blood and name comprise.

O'erlooking Adriatic Sea,
If fairer scene on earth there be,
It must be some gemmed crystal star,
To eclipse the charms of Mir-a-Mar.
Here Maximilian lived at peace
With all the world, and took his ease.
The blood of Cæsar through his veins,
(His brother Frank in Austria reigns),
Contented here to reign supreme;
With Charlotte, life passed as a dream.

The Sphinx got Mexicans to go
To tempt with crown of Mexico.
Oh! man whose youth has never read
That we by toil must earn our bread,
Who has not parable in mind
When Christ told Satan "get behind?"
These lessons, lost in Mir-a-Mar,
Commenced history of a fallen star.
The Cæsar's blood all scruples drown,
And he accepts the worthless crown.

Installed in Montezuma's halls,
He holds his court and gives his balls.
The rabble shout with loud acclaim,
Viva the Maximilian name!
The dirty throng, on turn of flood,
Will be the first to drink his blood.
'Twas ever so from Christ till now,
With people wallowing in the slough;
And he must drink the bitter cup,
Who ever tries to lift them up.

Carlotta's court was pure and good;
An empress, every inch, she stood.
Daughter of kings and queens as well,
She was, of all her courts, the belle.
Her ladies mostly came from France,
To seek in Mexico, romance,
And in the German's dirty messes
Some American adventuresses;
But those received most privily,
Were "Belgium's beauty and her chivalry."

Bazaine had quite his fortune made
By wedding wealthy native maid,
Whose sympathy at once came forth
To young ambassadress from the north;
And through her genuine support
I received the *entrée* into court,
And began to play my woman's part
To work the plans I had at heart.
I gave Bazaine a million francs,
Which he politely took, "with thanks."

He promised troops should issue forth
To take possession of the north.
The "Corps Belgique" was sent that way,
But only served to draw their pay.
They stopped along to drink their wine,
And never tried to cross the line.
The French troops lingered in each town,
Where cards and absinthe most abound.
The Emperor's rival, bold Bazaine,
Spoiled all by his desire to reign.

The Empress listened to my plaint,
And soothed me like a very saint.
"My child," she said, "come live with me,
And I will like a mother be.
I need one faithful friend at hand,
Not native of this treacherous land,
And yet with tongue and face extern
That sharpest spy cannot discern;
And more, I need myself about
One who with gold cannot be bought."

The empire spread from sea to sea,
Its flag protected bond and free;
And Maximilian was elate
A nation to regenerate.
One traitor thwarted all his plans,
Controlled his court, and tied his hands.
The Empress saw it very plain.
A rule like this was all in vain;
To rend this knot, the only chance
Was that she quickly go to France.

Again upon the treach'rous sea,
With ample escort, I and she.
In France her grandsire ruled, a king;
She comes a suppliant now, to bring
An Emperor's supplication near
The throne of one who cannot hear
Unless self-interest whets his ear.
The stone in Egypt's not more dumb,
The Sphinx itself is not more glum,
Than Bonapartes when Hapsburgs come.

We saw the cortege rolling out,
And heard the dirty rabble shout
"Vive l'Empereur!"—from palace-yard,
Along the gay-thronged boulevard.
The Sphinx sat in his coach of state;
Beside him sat his handsome mate.
Isis, Osiris, Nilus' gods,
O'er whom old hoary Egypt nods,
Transplanted here, less out of place
Than Corsican and Spanish race.

The Empress, crushed with her defeat,
Could neither now nor sleep nor eat;
Resolved to try another chance,
And see the greatest man in France—
Thiers had served her grandsire well—
And if mortal man could tell
The way to make Bazaine disgorge,
'Twas Wizard of the Place St. George,
For here long dwelt the State coquette,
Corner Rue Notre Dame de Lorette.

I went with her to Monsieur Thiers;
He was greatly moved by Charlotte's tears:
"My child, I loved your grandsire well;
He neglected my advice and fell.
Now this affair of Mexico
Gives Napoleon's empire its last blow;
He dances on a floor of glass;
This empire soon away must pass.
Recall your husband from afar,
And seek your home at Miramar."

My noble mistress, crushed with grief,
In floods of tears sought some relief.
"My child," she said, "one only hope,
And that to go and see the Pope.
The Holy Father sure must know
The need of saving Mexico.
Three hundred years a Christian land,
He must not yield it to the band
Of outlaws under Juarez's flag;
The Pope must issue forth his gag."

I wrote my chief a full account
Of what I here give dim recount,
And sent it, when I had it done,
By fastest mail to Washington,
In case they'd forced him to succumb,
And to the capital he'd come.
We had no other care in France;
The Pope was now our only chance,
Where flag of Christ was high unfurled,
Vicegerent of the Christian world.

In France, the spies around us crept;
The "Mouchards" watched our every step.
"Liberté, Egalité, Fraternité"—bah!
These only live in English law,
Where Queen and subject, each in place,
Form highest type of human race.
We passed through tunnel Mont Cenis,
And reached the plains of Italy,
The fairest land the sun shone on;
Her sons undying fame have won.

Arrived in Rome, Saint Peter's home,
Where Pio Nino holds the dome
Of Angelo, till Christ shall come.
All creeds pass by like filthy dross;
This creed is founded on the cross
Which Jesus, in his anguish, bore
To save the world for evermore.
With faith and hope divine—supernal,
He linked him to the world—fraternal,
That we should enter life eternal.

Established in our rooms of state,
I next upon my bankers wait.
A messenger, with profound salaam,
Hands me a cable telegram:

"WASHINGTON, April 15, 1867.

"ANITA, care of EYRE & MATTINI, Bankers, Rome:

"See Giulia Antonetti, 14 Montebello. She will introduce you to Baroness ———, Antonelli's mistress. Lavish money. Hope—Pope.

"4-15. Pd.   CHIEF."

This Giulia lived upon a street
Where evening promenaders meet,
And Roman lovers there arrange
Their salutations to exchange.
A little girl at window sat,
Each passing carriage gazing at,
And when the Cardinal passed by,
The child would always "Papa" cry.
The Antonetti was *passé*,
"Ancien maitresse," the French would say.

A little billet of exchange—
Convenient medium to arrange
A meeting with the Baroness,
And left with Giulia my address.
The Baroness spoke Spanish well,
Though what her race I could not tell.
Accomplished much in every art,
She gave the Cardinal her heart.
She promised at an early day
Assistance meet to pave the way.

The Antonetti's courtly grace
Excelled all courtly Latin race;
In tones as gentle as a child,
He soothed my fears in accents mild,
And gave assurance doubly sure,
The Pope would all dissensions cure,
And teach the upstart Bonaparte
A lesson that would wring his heart;
He pocketed a million francs,
And took his leave with "gracious thanks."

The Pope appointed soon a day
To have his ushers clear the way
To give the Empress audience,
And receive her due obedience.
When seated robed in Peter's chair,
He deigns all mortal plaints to hear;
Counsels faith, and hope, and charity,
And virtue of Christian rarity—
Only through him are sins forgiven;
He holds the very keys of heaven.

The Empress fell at Pius' feet,
And poured her plaint in tones so sweet
That Christ himself, had he been here,
Must needs in pity shed a tear.
She told her noble husband's wrongs:
How he was bound in Bazaine's thongs—
How Maximilian went for good—
How he and she had noble blood—
What plans they made on high to hoist
In Mexico the cross of Christ.

"My daughter, earth's of no avail;
I must the truth to you unveil:
Your noble husband's dead! On high
His soul reposes in the sky;
Intent alone on doing good,
The Mexicans have shed his blood."
A shriek, that Peter's dome had riven,
Ascended to the gates of heaven;
A soul the best God can create,
Has gone to heaven to join its mate.

The mind's the soul. When this departs,
Clay only forms the grosser parts.
The ethereal spirit comes from God;
It never rests beneath the sod.
In prison-house but for a day,
The soul oft longs to fly away;
To shake away the carnal dust,
And meet the spirits of the just;
To mount to heaven's distant blue,
And get the last eternal view.

In Schoenbrunn's noble palace walls,
In Francis Joseph's ancestral halls,
'Mid flowers, trees, and shrubbery hid,
My mistress lies an invalid.
The Austrian flag bears o'er the sea
What yet of Hapsburg's son there be,
To rest beneath the lofty spire
Of Kaiser's tomb in St. Sophia,
Where mausoleums of kingly great
Repose in dim, sepulchral state.

His hatchment hung,
His requiem sung,
We seek another change of scene,
And start for famed Ardennes green,
When Belgian lion rears his head
Above the mound of honored dead,
Who fighting, sturdy, brave, and true,
Gave up their lives at Waterloo;
Pointing his dexter arm at France—
Mute warning 'gainst an armed advance.

The Guelphs here hold their regal court,
In Belgium's capital and fort;
The sister of the reigning king
Comes home a broken heart to bring,
Where cannon thundered at her birth,
And she was blessed with all of earth.
The sight of Laaken's palace wood
May do the stricken sufferer good;
For here she played a little child,
When Nature all around her smiled.

In Brussels once I met a friend
Who stayed in Mexico to the end.
His mission there was education—
The last hope for regeneration.
A protegé of the house of Coburg,
The Abbe Seur Brasseur de Bourbourg.
He was Maxmilian's court librarian—
A famous Aztec antiquarian.
I sought advice from his strong mind,
A father's aid and counsel kind.

He said: All was lost of temporal power,
But Mexico was Mary's dower;
And no earthly power should wrest away
The richest gem in the Church's lay;
That Jesuit Order was ordained
To see that Mary's rights were gained;
That Father Beckh, a priest discreet,
Now filled the great Loyola's seat;
That he was now in Belgic land
Arranging a Western propagand.

That Mexico was not the whole:
America was now the goal.
The United States had equal laws,
Which were beneficial to the cause;
Enabling them, by education,
No doubt, ere long, to rule the nation,
For each political dispute
Advantage gives to the astute;
Then as crusaders we will go,
And repossess our Mexico.

Some Belgian nuns were about to start,
From Convent of the Sacred Heart,
By German Lloyds' ship "Pomona,"
To open schools in Arizona!
Mother Emerantia was lady superior,
Accompanied by ten inferior
Sisters—Hyacinth, Maximus, Ambrosia,
Monica, Martha, Mary, Euphrasia,
Lucretia, Francesca and Irene;
And I'm called Sister Seraphine.

The Abbé thought this was my chance;
There's nothing more to do in France,
And nothing can be done in Rome;
The Imperial troops are ordered home
At bid of the Republic North,
Which from the civil war came forth
Like giant who has tried his strength,
And found it equal to his length.
It stands colossal on two seas,
And fears not foreign enemies.

We soon arrived in fair New York,
And paid our dues to Central Park.
When driving through the upper part
To Convent of the Sacred Heart.
And while the party rested here,
I made a visit far more dear,
And went, accompanied by a nun,
To seek my chief in Washington.
He was to Arizona gone,
And I returned both sad and lone.

Another voyage on the sea—
God grant it be the last for me.
The old familiar southern star
Shone brightly over Panama;
The steamers still were wont to go
Along the coast of Mexico.
We passed in sight of old St. Luke,
And Sonora-land without a duke,
In safety landing men and freight,
In city of the Golden Gate.

Our mission first was Santa Clara,
To get the Bishop to prepare
Instructions for our journey on
To Arizona and Tucson.
Our party here received addition,
Two Jesuit fathers from the Mission—
Father Bosco, a native Frenchman,
The Italian Messia was his henchman.
The Jesuits always work in pairs,
The inferior blind obedience swears.

Again on sea we are afloat,
To Los Angeles by coastwise boat;
To Yuma, hence, a hundred leagues
Of desert, man and beast fatigues.
The ambulance out here is used
(The name it bears somewhat confused)
For transportation on the plains,
On deserts, and o'er mountain chains.
In this conveyance we took our seat,
And sailed along with the desert fleet.

The desert's glimmering mirage
Is likened only to the Taj,
In India raised 'tween earth and sky,
An architectural mystery:
A fleet of ships before our eyes,
Half-way between the earth and skies;
Their canvas spread with purple clouds,
Their flags all waving in the shrouds;
Then from our vision swift they flee
Like navy swallowed up at sea.

Then next a palace railway train
With flying banners scours the plain,
The snowy kerchiefs waving out
The windows; but we hear no shout.
Then just before a sea of glass
Obstructs the way, and stops the pass;
And on the other side the plain
Comes moving down another train,
Just like our own, to meet our own.
A moment—sea and train are gone.

The Yumas live in this precinct,
A race of Indians near extinct.
The white man's presence does no good;
They sell them rum for firewood,
Which steamboat-owners have to buy,
For boats that on the river ply.
The women lounge about the post;
The prettiest ones are soonest lost:
But this is somewhat delicate matter—
The less we say of it, the better.

While camped upon the river's bank,
A Yuma girl in illness sank,
And gave her gentle spirit up
From contact with the poisoned cup.
The chief came kindly to invite
Our party to the funeral rite.
The pyre was raised of mesquite wood;
At head of tomb the old chief stood;
The maid was stretched upon the pyre,
Which soon was wreathed by tongues of fire.

Her young companions stood around,
Their sorrow not evinced by sound,
But actions, louder far than words,
Proved their sincere and deep regards;
Each took some article of dress—
A handkerchief or bead necklace—
Some token of their childish games,
And with their sorrow fed the flames.
All worldly treasures now they spurn;
In silent sadness thus they mourn.

The Yumas are a stalwart race,
Erect in form and fair in face.
A full six feet the men would beat,
From tip to toe, in stocking-feet—
That is, if they but stockings wore;
But this incumbrance they ignore;
And custom also kindly grants
Unmentionable lack of pants.
Like other men who're better bred,
They mostly cultivate the head.

The river brings at highest flood
A sediment like Nilus' mud,
Enriching all it overflows;
The Yuma's pumpkin crop then grows.
In Congress once, to help these toilers,
My chief got a hundred thousand dollars,
To make in Colorado's val,
An irrigating canal.
The coin was in California spent
By a brother-in-law of the President.

This sediment the Yumas spread
In plaster thick upon the head,
Their dirty, long, black hair to scour,
And make "coif a la Pompadour."
'Tis said it long preserves the hair
From turning gray by age's wear;
Serves for a helmet in campaign;
From sun protects the Yuma brain.
Another thing not quite so nice,
It's sure to kill the—well, not rice.

In early days the women's dress
Was famous for its pliantness.
A cord between two trees was placed,
And tied to measure round the waist;
Then inner bark of cottonwood,
In ribbons long, and strong, and good,
Was doubled on the rope and tied,
The middle part made treble wide;
•For women's tastes are all the same
In Yuma maid or Paris dame.

The cord then tied around the waist,
The Yuma girl is quickly drest.
Her sylvan silk floats in the breeze,
And does not reach below the knees;
Impartial, too, above the waist
Her charms are left as Nature graced;
Then of her new-made costume proud,
She struts about among the crowd,
As every man must have a notion,
The very "poetry of motion."

But civilization's changed all this;
The flowing costume now you'll miss.
Red figured calico, grotesquer,
Supplants the undulating fresco,
Reaching above and below the knees.
The women lie and take their ease,
Exalted now above their sphere;
As is, perhaps, the case elsewhere.
They flirt, cajole, coquet, and wheedle
While men sit by and ply the needle.

Old Pasqual, chief of Yuma band,
And tallest man in Yuma land,
Was fond of loitering at the camp,
And took his spirits a little damp.
His coat was buttoned up before;
His hat on high gay plumage bore.
But lo! for his untutored mind,
His breeches were wrong side behind.
The jewel in toad's head, who knows?
Old Pasqual wears his in his nose.

The steamboat captain, bluff Wilcox,
Then anchored at the point of rocks,
Planned, for our company's diversion,
A complimentary excursion
To where the salt tide water flows,
The country of the Cocopas.
The Indians crowded on the decks,
To watch the engine's strange effects;
And when the engine blew off steam,
They jumped in fright into the stream.

The current here, six miles an hour,
Furnishes splendid water-power.
Before it reaches ocean's flood,
The Colorado's the color of blood,
And where the waters meet and clash,
The river's waters foam and dash;
Repressed by tide, strange it may seem,
New river's waters run up stream;
And where they meet in strife, galore,
Form in this land the greatest bore.

The Cocopas live near the mouth.
They have no rains, and yet no drouth.
In huts of tulé, firmly tied,
They rise and fall upon the tide.
Amphibious, as their name implies,
They live in water with gnats and flies.
Outlandish here they live on fish,
And spend a life somewhat rakish:
In dissipation, cards, and sloth,
Dressed in a little cotton cloth.

Returned from visit to the tide,
We anchored on the other side;
Just where the river's delta falls,
Below the Mission of St. Pauls;
Where Spanish priests in early days
Taught Yumas how to sing God's praise.
But they, perhaps for want of brains,
Killed all the priests to reward their pains.
We might go north, to the north pole;
But up the Gila is our role.

The map then had not, what a pity!
Been dignified by Gila City,
Reminding of the City of Peth,
Where one man lived, two starved to death.
Our first night was in "Mission Camp,"
Where the river-bed was somewhat damp;
For in former travels here I found
The rivers all run under ground.
This is a land of contradictions,
Involving one in endless fictions.

This camp was named for the commission
In early days sent on a mission,
When emigration first begun,
The nation's boundary to run,
Where Gila's waters ought to flow
Between the States and Mexico.
The commissary stores ran out,
The Com. himself was not about
(In writing always omit the Com.),
They broke up camp and started home.

Filibuster Camp next we reach,
This camp can moral lessons teach:
Some brave, strong men, long years ago,
From here invaded Mexico,
On promise made to them by greasers,
That they would fight like very Cæsars
To make republic in Sonora.
They met a death both swift and gory.
From this a useful lesson learn;
'Twixt whites and greasers quick discern.

We next pass peak of Antelope,
Where road with river has to cope;
Where once, in happy days gone by,
The harmless antelope could fly
From plains into the river's brink,
To quench its thirst with Gila's drink;
Where mountain goats on high could roam,
Surveying all around their home.
Now antelope or mountain goat
That venture here must risk a shot.

A long, dry ride, and longer walk,
From here to next place—Camp Mohawk.
Arriving at this misplaced name,
We found the scenery rather tame,
And turned around to take a view
Of scenery passed, ere entering new.
The Castle Dome looms in the north,
Like giant desert behemoth,
And western sun the vision thrills
O'er Yuma's gold and purple hills.

On south, the tenaja alta reigns,
The western boundary of the plains,
Whose tanks, formed out of solid rock,
In summer held the only stock
Of water in a hundred miles;
Whose serried edges and defiles
Accessible to mountain goat,
Or Mexicans who water tote
In leathern botas on long drives,
In desert lands to save their lives.

Next, Texas Hill looms on the plain.
Its summit we will never gain,
Nor base of scoria can surround,
Grim remnant of volcanic mound,
Forbidding, black, and desert ground.
What tales of horror here abound!
Fit place to murder and to rob;
The devil superintends the job.
He has not far away to roam,
For this looks like his very home.

The teamsters' camp we next approach,
And meet an overland stage-coach,
With mails and passengers, and news,
A desert treat which all diffuse;
Like ships when passing close at sea,
The desert has its courtesy.
A laguna on the southern bank
Forms convenient rendezvous and tank
For bathing in the summer day,
When train in hot noontide must stay.

At Stanwix Camp, we crossed the stream
To make a visit, like a dream,
Upon a fair Apache girl,
Of all her tribe the very pearl;
Who had abandoned her own race
To nestle here with a pale-face.
These two alone lived here alone,
And bid the robber Time begone,
Not counting year, nor month, nor sun,
And caring for no other one.

Agua Caliente, in Spanish called;
A spring that healed e'en those who crawled
To bathe their limbs in its warm waters;
For years used by Apache daughters,
As Indian maidens' charm divine
To make their skin as velvet fine.
The old, wild feeling came again
To strip and plunge me in the bain,
And there in bath, like two giours,
Marie and I talked on for hours.

We talked of old Apache camp,
And things that sounded rather damp
To ears polite from Europe's courts,
So different from Apache sports;
Of wars and all of war's alarms;
Of Apache wrongs, Apache harms;
Of wedded life, and how it went,
And how the days and nights were spent;
And last, not least, to assuage my grief,
I asked Marie about my chief.

She said he'd come with high commission
To settle the Indians' condition,
And passed along the Gila way,
With train and troops in grand array;
Had called to talk with her and G.
About old times, perhaps 'bout me;
That tales came down the river road
Of quarrels high, and strife, and blood,
And great dissensions among the whites
About the cause of Indian fights;

That new men came to make more bother,
Knew not one Indian from another;
That afterwards she heard from Burks
By one of Col. King Woolsey's clerks:
He'd gone down the road in angry mood,
And left the place at last for good;
E'en had not called in passing by,
To pay salutes, or say good-by.
I turned away at this surprise,
Suspended talk, and washed my eyes.

I lay musing in the limpid bath,
Upon life's strange and winding path;
My hair down—flowing to my waist,
My heaving bosom to embrace.
The buoyant water exposed to view
My rounded limbs, and shadows threw,
Pellucid twins, into the stream,
Which washed away life's dearest dream.
I robed my heavy bosoms' swell,
And bade Marie a kind farewell.

We crossed the river at Burks's ford,
And passed along the mesa road,
To where a hollow on the plat
The history marks of Oatman Flat.
In eighteen hundred and fifty-two
A traveler could have had this view:
An emigrant struggling up the hill,
His wife and children the wagon fill.
The Tontos following on his track,
The moment seized for fierce attack.

The husband's brains soon strew the road,
The wife and children dead are strewed;
Save two girls, whose lives are saved,
And Indian captives they are made.
A boy left for dead upon the road,
Was found by Pimas who that way rode,
And nursed by these Samaritans
(Who are falsely called barbarians),
With tenderness and care quite human,
Till he was fit to send to Yuma.

The girls were carried to the north,
From whence the Tonto band came forth,
To mountains where the mixed tribes range,
And in course of time, by fair exchange,
From desert plains and beds of lava,
To richer valley of Mohave,
Where, as Indian vague tradition saith,
The younger one succumbed to death.
Her sister Olive feared her knell,
But she was rescued by Grinnell.

A grave in sad and lonely place,
A little fence of stones embrace—
Made by some voyagers on the plains—
All that was found of their remains.
The scene accorded with my heart:
Each plays in life his fated part;
In desert lands some find their graves,
And some in death the deep-sea laves.
My contemplation's rather blue,
For I have been a captive too.

The Painted Rocks claim notice next,
All covered o'er with Indian text,
In hieroglyphic bows and clubs,
To pose some antiquarian Stubbs;
But versed somewhat in Indian lore
From education heretofore,
I read the signs as treaties made
By tribes, each other not to raid.
From Yuma lands to Pima's mound,
'Tis monumental half-way ground.

Arrived at last at Gila bend,
Our river journey comes to end.
'Tis wise to stop here wheels to tauter,
To rest, and fill the cans with water,
And prepare the mules the trip to stand
O'er Maricopa Desert's sand.
'Tis forty miles, or forty-five,
To where a human being can live;
And as there's always ample light,
'Tis best to cross it in the night.

The Maricopa wells we gain,
And turn to graze the weary train;
For here in peace and calm content
The Maricopas lives are spent.
A people stalwart, brave, and frank,
Driven from Colorado's bank
By intestine wars, long years ago,
They here in peace and plenty sow—
A kind of desert fringe œdemous,
Affiliated with the Pimas.

The women friendly, full of humor,
Were somewhat darker than the Yuma;
Wore cotton strips around the waist—
I judge they are not very chaste.
The men, a brave and honest race,
Stalwart in form and strong in face.
The chief, among them greatest man,
Came with a paper in his hand,
Unfolded from a buckskin roll,
And stood for us to read the scroll.

UNITED STATES SUPERINTENDENCY OF INDIAN AFFAIRS
FOR ARIZONA.

JANUARY 10, 1864.

This is to certify that Juan Chivarea is the recognized captain and chief of the MARICOPA tribe of Indians. All officers and citizens of the United States are respectfully requested to treat him as such.

CHARLES D. POSTON,
Superintendent.

(Seal)

From here above for twenty miles
The Pima cultivation smiles.
You do not see it by the road;
The river's bank is their abode.
Arrived at Pima Agent's Station,
A little time for purification.
I was rejoiced here to find
Heh-wul-vopuey, the Running Wind;
My maid, my sister, captive friend.
We embrace again before the end.

Along the river bank we walked,
And talked, and talked, oh, how we talked!
'Twas doubtful which was greatest talker.
She told me she was Mrs. Walker;
That a young and good American
Had come among the tribe to train
The young idea how to shoot,
And had won her hand, and heart to boot.
She was happy as the day was long,
And always thought the world was young.

The agent here, old Ammie White,
Gave us a comfortable night.
He spread our beds with Pima quilts,
And walked about like one on stilts.
His long legs working like a lever
(In youth he'd had the spindle fever).
A man of cultivated mind,
He lived a recluse from mankind,
Contented here in this Utopia
To spend life with a Maricopa.

Two men lived here about the yards
Well worth in passing some regards.
One wore a continental hat,
Somewhat the worse for wear at that,
A bullet-hole shot through the crown
Received in battle of Yorktown;
The other, a suit of buckskin clothes,
Red hair, and long, red, shining nose;
And both so cross-eyed, was the pother,
They never once saw one another.

The fathers would not Sabbath pass
Without celebrating Pima mass.
The Indians gathered all around,
With gaping wonder, on the ground,
And heard that God lived in the sky,
And fed good Indians pumpkin pie;
But bad ones sent to another place,
Where water's said to be rather scarce;
Exciting thus their hopes and fears
For the first time in three hundred years.

Having finished this, the train passed on
Along the road towards Tucson.
Leaving the stream at Sacaton
(Named from a grass of Arizone),
We camped a night at old Picach—
A peak for which you'll scarce find match;
Next rested at the point of rocks
Where Tucson keeps her herds and flocks;
And next day, near the time of noon,
We reached the plaza of old Tucson.

Kind friends soon come round to greet;
Some old we miss, some new we meet
(For Time must always have his scope);
The world's a vast kaleidoscope.
The flag again is here unfurled;
They think this the center of the world;
For London neither know nor care—
Four thousand here, four millions there;
Know nothing of stocks and "contangos;"
They play and sing and hold fandangos.

The Tucson people were quite elate,
They'd swapped the capital for a delegate;
All for this exalted honor itch,
And would swap the devil for a witch;
The governor has this condition,
·He signs the delegate's commission,
And for the honor and the pelf,
He always signs it for himself.
The Washington folks here might learn
Advantage of the count to turn.

LITH.BRITTON, REV 4 CO.S.F.

I'm not versed in affairs of state,
And politics I really hate;
But woman's instinct oft discerns
What man's more matchless reason spurns.
The best built coach that rides the plains,
Is n't safe if a drunkard holds the reins;
The strongest ship may go to wreck
With a land-lubber on the quarter-deck;
If neither happen, 'tis not odd;
But due to providence of God.

New men had come upon the scene
Not much better than the old, I ween.
They had a lean and hungry look;
In ravenous haste their victuals took
Down slim intestinal canal
With gustatory pleasure dismal;
Talked nasally about the flag,
And carried one in their carpet-bag;
Reckoned as how an acre of land
Was quite enough for any man.

Pile up the debt—who the d——l cares,
We'll leave this blessing to our heirs.
"The desert lands" must be surveyed,
And party-men three prices paid.
The Indian business pays us well,
The Quakers all may go to h——l.
The outsiders can't make a fuss,
The newspapers all belong to us;
Anything to save the nation,
"The old flag and an appropriation."

Our Lord-ly treasurer must have funds,
For finance low at the capital runs;
And what would Washington lobby be
Without some money to spend? He! he!
For every office has its price,
And the salaries don't half suffice;
So collect the duties on import,
We must keep up a friend at court.
The President has got the cranks,
And will no more submit to pranks.

We bought this land from Santa Ana
When he sold out under the hammer.
The old, one-legged Peter Funk!
Ten millions must have made him drunk.
The treaty made with old Gadsden
Was all very well, as things went then.
For old titles now we've no regards—
We've become a nation of communards;
We'll confiscate these old estates,
And then make tracks for Eastern States.

The bold frontiersman too was gone
(At least not seen about Tucson),
Who erst, with pistol on his hip,
With rifle true, and spur and whip,
Was ready for an Apache ride,
To do his best, whate'er betide.
Now, blear-eyed drunkards with their boons
Crowd low-down gambling-house saloons,
And hospitality's wide-spread gates
Are closed 'gainst strangers from the States.

The agent left at Arivac,
Soon as the owner turned his back,
Commenced to steal and confiscate,
And wreck and rob the whole estate;
Employed some dirty peon hands
To take it up as "desert lands;"
And with the treasury at his back
Would be the Lord of Arivac.
The name of this despicable fraud
Would nearly rhyme with DOCTOR LORD.

A few days' rest in old Tucson,
Then three leagues thence we journeyed on
To place in mem'ry always dear;
The Mission Church of San Xavier,
Where Indians long their vigils kept
(The church was clean and neatly swept).
For the Jesuits told them years ago,
Sure as the water would continue to flow,
The sun to shine, the grass to grow,
They'd come again to the Papago.

And now we've surely lived to see
Fulfillment of this prophecy;
And more: The time's not very far—
By treaty, purchase, or by war,
By means which nothing can forego—
We'll repossess our Mexico.
No earthly power can thwart the skill
Of an army moved by a single will.
And Mexico shall be our home,
Whene'er the order comes from Rome.

We left the fathers here to chaunt,
To teach the Indians how to plant,
By honest labor to serve H. I. M.,
And at eve to sing the vesper hymn;
Whilst we, too, render our account
By teaching on Saint Joseph's Mount.
And I in spirits desperate
Begin my own novitiate:
On condition, which Rome's law allows,
In future to withdraw my vows.

My chief was gone, and none knew where.
Suffice for me, he was not here.
Some said he'd wandered to Japan;
Others, the city of the Khan,
Or away beyond the Chinese wall,
On Scythian plains to build a kraal,
'Mid Tartar nomads living there
As their descendants live out here,
In ancient home of the Apache,
Where Russians now hold Fort Kiach'ta;

Or, fanned by India's spicy breeze,
To seek an island in the seas.
But I know best his tastes and wants,
The kind of scene his vision haunts;
He'll seek the island of Ceylon,
And spend a little time upon
The lore and creed of Buddhist monks,
Neath banyan trees' time-honored trunks;
Then cross the narrow Indian Sea,
From British port Trincomalee.

Then up fair India's coral strands
To where the Ganges spreads her sands;
In India's marble palaces,
To drink from Hindoo chalices;
To climb the hundred marble stairs
From Ganges' banks to old Benares,
Great city of the Hindoo mind,
Seat of the learned and refined;
Where pundits reason of the soul;
Below the healing waters roll.

Cawnpore, Lucknow, and high Delhi,
Where now the British banners fly,
At topmost top of Mogul towers,
In proud disdain of Moslem powers;
Where sixteen cities on the plain
Have risen, flourished, and fallen again;
Where Kootab tower and minaret
Stands tallest tower erected yet;
Where wrote England's poet of beauty and bliss:
"If there's an elysium on earth, it is this, it is this."

The Mogul's city, Agra, seek
And linger there at least a week,
By wonder architectural
Eclipsing all; the Taj Mahal.
Tribute of love by India's Khan,
The Mogul Emperor Shah Jehan,
In honor of wife best loved of all—
The beauteous Tartar, Noor-Mahal.
The Saracen here sought to prove
In showers of gems his lofty love.

It may be some bright crystal star
Descended from the realms afar,
To give of home conception dim,
Of cherubim and seraphim;
Or, perhaps, the genii of the seas
Have wafted here, mankind to please,
A palace fashioned in the deep,
From gems which ocean's treasuries keep,
Festooned with coral, heap on heap,
In which the mermaids sing and sleep.

The marble, too, here speaks to man,
Inlaid in each verse of Koran;
In precious stones each Indian flower
Is molded in sepulchral bower;
So lifelike they the tomb illume,
You fancy you can smell perfume;
And look above in dome, on wing
To hear the very angels sing—
A poem here in marble wove—
Earth's noblest monument of love!

The Himalayas' highest peak,
In adventure wild I'm sure he'll seek,
The natural British-Indian wall,
O'erlooking Thibet and Nepaul;
Where Ganges, fed by lasting snows,
Its sources finds and southward flows;
The west and south all British land,
The north and east all Turkestan,
In clouds where Asian eagles whirl,
O'er Ararat survey the world.

He often read to me Tom Moore
In secluded, happy days of yore.
Following this, in mem'ry dear,
He'll visit valley of Cashmere.
Where mountains fifteen thousand feet
Rise, top o'er top, the skies to meet;
And I fear on Jhelung's happy waters
He'll sport with Cashmere's lovely daughters.
To love and beauty men incline—
I am the first, I'll not repine.

The Hindoo Kush he'll push across,
And rest among the Persian floss,
Where maidens fairer than Cashmere,
Would make an anchorite forswear.
But he has holier, higher aims,
And will seek the mystic Persian flames
Which burn there since the world begun,
'Mid ancient worshipers of the sun;
From Ispahan to India's shore,
God's greatest emblem they adore.

Then up the great Euphrates' banks,
Where Moslem mezzuin prays and chants
Above the ruined cities old—
Oh! how old! buried in the mold
Of ages ere the Christian world
From Bethlehem the flag unfurled,
Which Magian priests went there to seek
On birth of Christ, in obedience meek,—
Thank Herod, who then held sway,
It did not take an eastern way.*

---
*Herod drove the Magian priests out of Judea; else they would probably have carried the Christian religion eastward.

The Holy Land! the Holy Land!
Like Arizona, land of sand!
Where prophet sage and paraclete
The face of eternal God can greet;
Where atmosphere, without a leaven,
Leaves naught betwixt the earth and heaven.
Where soul absorbs th' ethereal spark,
And leaves the outer world in dark.
Her sands have drunken Christe's blood,
To save the world beyond the flood.

On pyramid by Nilus' bank,
Where Egypt's lotus leaves grow dank,
The river winding through Soudan
Forms nature's desert caravan;
Comes whence Herodotus too soon
Placed source in Mountains of the Moon;
Whence Livingstone and Stanley meet,
And strangers, yet like brothers greet.
The one takes rest up in the sky,
The other solves the mystery.

O'er Europe's lands no more we'll roam,
Globe-trotters make them summer home.
Oh, will my chief not ever come?
My bankers wrote he'd passed through Rome,
And called to get a small advance
From money in the Bank of France.
I fear he's caught in some foulards
Which flaunts upon the boulevards,
Societé damsels dressed so nice
Upon the wages of their vice.

Some men from London after came,
With power to enter in his name
The Santa Rita mining claims.
(I purposely omit their names,
For some of them are " unco quid,"
And would not steal if understood.)
But agents do for filthy gains
Re-enter claims in their own names.
I must confess, I have my fears
Of "eminent mining engineers."

They brought along some magazines,
Of introduction forming means,
With tales of frontier life and fight
No other man on earth could write.
I knew the old sarcastic style,
The lightly veiled sardonic smile;
The scenes descriptive like a picture,
The ethics of the "Parsee Lecture;"
But still my heart full often wonders
Why he so long should stay in Londres.

They said he loved the English law,
Which can keep thieves somewhat in awe.
In English home had liked to nestle,
Where each man's house is as his castle;
And thought the English right to fight
For the old motto, " Dieu et mon droit;"
Is quite at ease in English homes,
And welcome guest at feast he comes;
But worse than all, eternal Hades!
I fear he loves the English ladies.

At last the news reached old Tucson
That he had come to Washington
To spend the winter with old friends;
To watch the count on which all depends;
To join the dinner, ball, and rout,
Which in season rages thereabout.
The spring brought me the joyful tidings
That he had finished all his ridings—
Was home again, in land of sands,
As Government Register of Lands.

The capital again on wheels
Has left the southern broad grain-fields,
To rest in Prescott 'mong the pines,
And live upon the yield of mines;
The Governor there to practice law,
And bail his clients with men of straw,
Unless the President interdict;
To pardon give his own convict;
To colonize the land with blacks,
Be delegate and then make tracks.

From Florence City to San Xavier,
Three different styles the buildings wear;
Three different epochs, different races,
Have left their marks in these old places:
The Mission Church, in art and grace,
Stands high above the rest in place;
The style is from the Saracen,
The dome a type of the Unseen;
Half Christian church, half Moslem mosque,
With ornaments in Arabesque.

CASA GRANDE

The Casa Grande stands alone,
One league from road from old Tucson,
Sole monument in desert place
Of lost, extinct, and perished race
Who here some thousand years ago
Had hate and love and joy and woe,
And cultivated lands around,
And built a city—now a mound.
No other nation 'neath the sun
Would let this ruin, to ruin run.

They say a thousand years ago
The Gila's waters ceased to flow;
The Great Spirit, wroth, withheld the rain,
And Indians no more gathered grain.
The queen had garnered the little corn,
And eked it out as a child was born
Till at last of humans under the sun
She was the only living one,
And reposed herself beneath a tree,
To wake up in eternity;

That God, in pity, sent the rain,
The human race to yet maintain—
A drop from heaven fell on her navel,
The womb of nature to unravel,
And virgin queen, without deception,
Accepted the divine conception.
In course of time a son was born,
And Indians again danced 'round their corn;
The queen undying honor won—
Grandmother of Montezuma's son.

Fair Florence, wreathed in Gila's green,
A city yet to be, I ween.
Green cottonwoods adorn the banks,
Mesquite for food and fuel ranks;
And nowhere 'neath Italia's sun
Can climate equal such a one.
The territorial cord spinál
Spreads here in many a branch canal,
To irrigate the fields of grain,
And make good crops come without rain.

The water, trained in living rills,
The sidewalk's pine-built channel fills,
Vivifying the umbrageous trees
'Neath which they sit, and take their ease;
For here, e'en more than in Tucson,
It is always, "always afternoon."
The lotus leaf the soft wind kisses,
And ladies here would charm Ulysses.
They spend their time in dance and song,
And seem happy as the day is long.

The Gila's silvery waters flow
Through the town as classic old Arno
Flows through fair Italia's Firenze,
Enough to give a poet frenzy.
The glittering floods in fancy seem
A silver thread in fringe of green.
The churches yet are rather few,
The ethics of the country new;
If not devout, they're cousin-german—
A murderer preached the funeral sermon.

The Pinal range ten leagues to north
Is where the silver ores come forth.
Here, well preserved in womb of Nature,
In mountain summits' wild serrature,
Mysterious Providence has kept
His richest treasures in the depth
Of Apache-land, for chosen vessels,
Who in prayer with great Jehovah wrestle;
For pious, good, God-fearing men—
Who drink a little now and then.

In truth, this mountain range it seems
With richest minerals really teems,
And silver ores of richest ley
Are hauled away from day to day,
To reduction works in other lands.
Four dollars a day are paid to hands.
This treasury, in years to come,
Will make Florence a great emporium.
The Italian has the Apennines,
But they contain no silver mines.

I rested here from my fatigue,
And spent a day with his colleague;
A brusquely military man,
In point of years about the span;
A wife intent on household cares,
Somewhat his junior in years.
Two little girls born in Florence;
One Flora named, the other Florence.
I asked him why so near the same?
He answered, To prevent nickname.

About a league northwest of town,
A round butte rises from the ground;
Alone it stands upon the plain,
Detached from ev'ry mountain chain;
In altitude three hundred feet,
The morning sun's first beams to greet.
Its evening's shadows fall apace
In eastern alcove, which forms place
For building a secluded home
Where one may wait life's coming gloam.

On eastern front an Apache cave,
In solid rock sepulchral nave,
Forms tomb to face the rising sun,
For place of rest when life is done;
On top a temple built of stone,
For worship of the GREAT UNKNOWN;
Resembling those on Persian hills,
Which Zoroaster's follower builds;
And sacred fire burns constantly,
As type of immortality.

On high a lofty pine is raised,
And on its top a flag is placed;
Not nailed to mast, as heroes do;
Nor lashed with ropes, as sailor's clew;
But always to the breeze it flings,
Revolving around on iron rings;
Red sun in midst, blue border round,
A stout white canvas forms the ground.
For fifty miles around you view
The colors true, "red, white, and blue."

We cross the river at the spot
Where long ago it was our lot
To be rescued from our willow boat
By Pimas planting thereabout.
Now, lo! a city on the plains,
Where smiling peace and plenty reigns,
Named for the fabled bird that dies
That another from its death may rise;
Immortal emblem, long, long float
O'er PHŒNIX, where Pimas saved our boat!

My story now draws near the end.
The few remaining words attend:
We offer here ourselves as guides,
To go with you, whate'er betides;
We know the river's winding way,
The cataract's unceasing play;
The cañon's deep and narrow gorge,
Where whirlpools dangerous roar and surge,
The rocks on which your boat may split,
The river, every bit of it.

And more, if more I need to urge,
A woman's heart beats 'neath this serge
(Which courtesy and chivalry
Respect, as heaven's livery),
For one who's gone aboard the boat,
These many years the world afloat;
Whose guide and comfort I would be
Over life's remaining troubled sea,
Till anchored safe at last with me
On the shores of vast eternity.